Magical Musical Kingdom

FRANCES S. TURNBULL

Published by Musicaliti® Publishers
575 Tonge Moor Road, Bolton, BL2 3BN

Copyright © 2013 Musicaliti®
ISBN 978-1-907935-15-2
Printed in the USA
All rights reserved. No part of this publication may be reproduced, stored in a retrieval system, or transmitted by any means, mechanical, photocopying, recording or otherwise, without the prior permission of the copyright holder.

CONTENTS

	Introduction	v
	Curriculum Detail	vi
	What you will need	vii
	What it sounds like	viii
	Activity Planner	x
1	King and Queen	13
2	Knight and Lady	23
3	Princess and Prince	33
4	Goblin and Fairy	43
5	Dragon and Unicorn	53
6	Summary Weeks	63
7	Handouts	67
8	Musicaliti Characters	78
9	Make your own Rhythms	80

MAGICAL MUSICAL KINGDOM: NURSERY SERIES
INTRODUCTION

Musicaliti® is about S.P.A.C.E.

SPACE is an acronym that we use to describe the elements in every Musicaliti® session.

Sing:
We sing before we play on the instruments, because:
Singing provides immediate feedback and shows understanding.

Play:
We play games and instruments every time, because:
Games are fun and easily hold attention because they depend on responding immediately!

Act:
We act out the story or characters, because:
Acting develops empathy and helps to develop subtle changes in dynamics like loud and quiet.

Create:
We create our own music, because:
Understanding and creating original music shows true musicality.

Explore:
We explore new ways to make sounds, because:
Improvisation is the ability to respond musically to a feeling or story.

SPACE statements are research-based reasons for the activities we do. Using the acronym SPACE, these areas highlight the essential areas of child development and provide an explanation of the benefits of the selected activities.

Social:
The welcoming greeting routine prepares children for a new activity as well as demonstrating a better way to start the day/session.

Physical:
Including whispering, speaking and singing allows children to experiment with communication.

Academic:
Developing sensitive listening helps children to respond better to instruction and detail.

Creative:
Teaching patterns develops children spatial planning and awareness.

Emotional:
Routine provides emotional security by knowing what to expect.

FRANCES S. TURNBULL

Musicaliti® means learning for life

Musicaliti® is the complete creative curriculum for children from birth to 7.

Age	0-1 year	1-2 years	2-3 years	3-4 years	4-5 years	5-6 years	6-7 years
Awards	Red	Orange	Yellow	Green	Blue	Purple	Violet
In a circle children can:	Sit and sway	Sit and tap knees	Hold hands, walk	Play circle games	Step and step back	Inner and outer circles	Dance with inner circle
Listening to music, children can:	Eyes follow movement	Eyes follow movement	Copy actions	Copy actions	Play partner games	Play partner games	Conduct songs in 2/4
When leaving the last song line out, children can:	Show surprise	Continue song thru movement	Continue song vocally	Sing the last phrase	Sing the last 2 phrases	Sing the missing motif	Clap beat of missing motif
Children can use:	Shaking instrument	Tapping instrument	Drum and beater	Triangle and beater	Cymbal and beater	Glockenspiel (2 notes)	Ukulele (2 strings)
Children use language by:	Pointing at things	Pointing at body parts	Acting song characters	Acting song characters	Understanding clever lyrics	Acting diff. characters	Perform song in character
In a line, children can:	Roll over	Walk in pairs	Follow in a line	Follow in a spiral	Walk in line, creating bridges	Walk in a snail and undo it	Walk in line with partners
Children recognise:	Crotchet	Crotchet	Crotchet, Quaver	Crotchet, Quaver	Crotchet, Quaver, Dotted rhythm	Crotchet, Quaver, Dotted, rhythm	Crotchet, Quaver, Dotted, rhythm, Minim
Children recognise:	Minor 3rd (E-C or sol-mi)	Minor 3rd (E-C or sol-mi)	Perfect 5th (A-F# or sol-mi)	Major 6th (B-A or sol-la)	Major 3rd (F#-D or mi-doh)	Major 2nd (E-D or re-doh)	Octave (D''-D' or doh''-doh')
Children match the pitch by:	Bouncing up (E) and down (C)	Jumping up (E) and down (C)	Touching shoulders (F#) and hips (D)	Shoulders (A)-head (B)	Hips (F#)-toes (D)	Knees (E)-toes (D)	Over head (D'')-toes (D')
Children keep the pulse through:	Clapping	Stamping	Flick/ clicking	Hopping	Skipping	Patsching (knee tap)	Variety of methods
Singing range:	a'-a''	a'-a''	d'-b'	c'-c''	d'-d''	d'-d''	d'-d''
Children can	3/5 songs	6/10 songs	11/20	12/28	16/35 songs	22/42	28/50
Weekly sessions:	10 min	10 min	15 min	20 min	30 min x 2	45 min	45 min

In every subject, we develop skills incrementally, from easy to complex. The same is true in music, so we use physical activity to introduce complex skills, from bouncing and rolling over, to walking and skipping, to writing music notation.

The Musicaliti® series provides activities to support the musical development of children from birth until they are physically strong and mentally experienced enough to hold and play musical instruments, in turn developing their other learning areas like maths and reading.

MAGICAL MUSICAL KINGDOM: NURSERY SERIES

What you will need:

Nursery Week 1 & 2

Weeks 1 and 2:
CD/iPod, scarves, drums, shaker, character pictures, stickers

Weeks 3 and 4:
CD/iPod, sticks, chime bar, character pictures, stickers

Weeks 5 and 6:
CD/iPod, sand blocks, bells, character pictures, stickers

Weeks 7 and 8:
CD/iPod, shakers, bells, scarves, character pictures, stickers

Weeks 9 and 10:
CD/iPod, triangle, sand blocks, drum, sticks, character pictures, stickers

Weeks 11 and 12:
CD/iPod, character pictures and instruments depending on the songs chosen

FRANCES S. TURNBULL

What it sounds like:

What is a beat (or pulse)?
In music, a beat (is the ongoing tap or clap in a song. It can be thought of as the 'heartbeat' of the song because this is what keeps the song going, usually by the low instruments. You can hear the beat of any song by walking to it. It is even-paced, usually taking the same length of time as the next tap or clap, and does not usually match the words or tune of the song. It can even sound a little boring, e.g. 'twinkle, twinkle, little star' or 'bee-bee-bee-bee'.

What is a rhythm?
In music, a rhythm is a group of notes together. Sometimes it is repeated by percussion instruments (shaking/tapping/scraping), so that all through the song, you hear 'cup of tea - cup of tea -', or like the insect notes below, 'spider-bee, spider-bee'. It is also the tune or words/lyrics of the song, e.g. 'twinkle, twinkle, little star' or 'spider-spider-spider-bee'.

NOTE/RHYTHM (basic)	MOVEMENT	WORD SOUND	INSECT PICTURE
o semibreve	ve-ry slow walk 1 - - - *long*	4 counts snai-ai-ai-il	snail
𝅗𝅥 minim	slow walk 1 - *long*	2 counts wo-rm	worm
♩ crotchet	walk 1 *step*	1 count bee	bee
♫ quaver	jog-ging 1-2 *step-step*	1 count spi-der	spider
semiquaver	jog-ging quick-ly 1 - 2 - 3 - 4 *short-short-short-short*	1 count ca-ter-pil-lar	caterpillar

What it sounds like:

Nursery Week 1 & 2

Why move to music?
In many cultures, the word music means 'dance and sound', because in all cultures, music composers are inspired by movement. When we can experience a rhythm or a beat, we learn it inside-out, and are able to repeat it over again without needing to think about it. Moving to music is also the most effective behaviour control, demanding the attention of all faculties, as well as giving the teacher immediate feedback on individual student understanding.

Why use pictures and words?
Using pictures, words or even rhythm sounds (ta, ti-ti etc) are bridges to understanding notation, and just as we all have different learning styles, these are yet another form of bridge. You may find children that prefer to use notation straight away, or prefer alternative bridges that don't hold specific meaning - the only time it is wrong is if it leads to incorrect or inaccurate understanding, which is seen instantly in the singing, playing or performance of the song.

NOTE/RHYTHM (basic)	MOVEMENT	WORD SOUND	INSECT PICTURE
dotted quaver semiquaver	skip-ty 1 - 2 *long-short*	1 count bee-tle	*beetle*
semiquaver dotted quaver	gal-lop 1 - 2 *short-long*	1 count the-ant	*ant*
triplet	tri-ple run 1 - 2 - 3 *jog-jog-jog*	1 count but-ter-fly	*butterfly*
quaver-semiquaver-semiquaver	jog quick-ly 1 - 2 - 3 *long-short-short*	1 count ham - bur-ger	*hamburger*
semiquaver-semiquaver-quaver	quick-ly jog 1 - 2 3 *short-short-long*	1 count sau-sa-ges	*sausages*

FRANCES S. TURNBULL

Magical Musical Kingdom Activity Planner

Nursery Week 1&2

Activity	Week 1:	Week 2:	Week 3:	Week 4:	Week 5:	Week 6:
Hello Song	Whispering Voice	Whispering Voice	Whispering Voice	Whispering Voice	Whispering Voice	Whispering Voice
Physical Warm Up	Old King Glory	Old King Glory	Knight and Horse	Knight and Horse	Semiquaver	Semiquaver
Vocal Warm Up	I am King	I am King	Duke of York	Duke of York	Built my princess	Built my princess
Instrument Play	Queens of Hearts	Queens of Hearts	Down came my friend	Down came my friend	Little Bells	LIttle Bells
Pattern Dance	Queens are Royal	Queens are Royal	Pink Hat	Pink Hat	Hopping Hopping	Hopping Hopping
Story	King Crotchet	Queen Quaver	Knight Quaver	Lady Minim	Princess Semiquaver	Frog-Prince
Body Percussio	Clear Air	*	*	*	*	*
Rhythm	*	Cattails	*	*	*	*
Tempo	*	*	Indended Force	*	*	*
Dynamics	*	*	*	Relent	*	*
Free Dance	*	*	*	*	Electrodoodle	*
Instrument Pass	*	*	*	*	*	Divertisse-ment
Craft ideas	Crowns, Stickers	Sceptre, Stickers	Armour, Stickers	Coat of Arms,	Rings	Hopping frogs
Goodbye Song	Goodbye my friends	Goodbye my friends	Goodbye my friends	Goodbye my friends	Goodbye my friends	Goodbye my friends

* The lesson arrangement matches the teaching CD/download which is planned for a 30 minute music session. You may prefer to use the instrumental music to develop a different skill depending on your group, or to extend the session beyond 30 minutes.

MAGICAL MUSICAL KINGDOM: NURSERY SERIES

Magical Musical Kingdom Activity Planner

Nursery Week 1&2

Activity	Week 7:	Week 8:	Week 9:	Week 10:	Week 11:	Week 12:
Hello Song	Whispering Voice	Whispering Voice	Whispering Voice	Whispering Voice	Whispering Voice	Whispering Voice
Physical Warm Up	Goblin	Goblin	Dragon	Dragon	King	King
Vocal Warm Up	Goblin Protector	Goblin Protector	Do pity my case	Do pity my case	Queen	Queen
Instrument Play	Love Somebody	Love Somebody	Dragon and the Unicorn	Dragon and the Unicorn	Knight	Knight
Pattern Dance	Skipping Flying	Skipping Flying	Beautiful Unicorn	Beautiful Unicorn	Lady	Lady
Story	Goblin	Flying Fairy	Dragon	Unicorn	Princess	Princess
Body Percussion	Music to Delight	*	*	*	Prince	Prince
Rhythm	*	Poofy Reel	*	*	Goblin	Goblin
Tempo	*	*	One-eyed Maestro	*	Fairy	Fairy
Dynamics	*	*	*	Happy Alley	Dragon	Dragon
Free Dance	*	*	*	*	Unicorn	Unicorn
Instrument Pass	*	*	*	*	Electrodoodle	Electrodoodle
Craft ideas	Goblin ears Stickers	Fairy Wings Stickers	Dragon spikes	Unicorn horn, stickers	Stickers, handouts	Stickers, handouts
Goodbye Song	Goodbye my friends	Goodbye my friends	Goodbye my friends	Goodbye my friends	Goodbye my friends	Goodbye my friends

* The lesson arrangement matches the teaching CD/download which is planned for a 30 minute music session. You may prefer to use the instrumental music to develop a different skill depending on your group, or to extend the session beyond 30 minutes.

MAGICAL MUSICAL KINGDOM: NURSERY SERIES

Nursery Week 1&2

1 KING & QUEEN

King Crotchet
We begin our musical adventure by focusing on the regular beat or pulse of the crotchet. In this series, we compare the crotchet to walking normally, and we use different songs and activities to emphasise the continuity of the regular beat: "and the beat goes on". We also personify the characteristics of this note as King Crotchet, the strong and stately ruler of the Magical Musical Kingdom, who is not in a hurry to go anywhere, but walks carefully and with his head held up high. This description encourages both walking to the beat of the song as well as correct posture when walking.

Queen Quaver
The second half of the session contrasts the regular beat of walking with quicker steps for jogging as we introduce Queen Quaver. She is described as someone always moving twice as quickly than the King, and as we introduce even quicker notes later on (semiquavers), it is important to show a clear difference between jogging and running quickly (later topic).

Timing
As the session leader, it is important that when you contrast the King/Queen activities, you demonstrate steps accurately, fitting two evenly-spaced jogging steps in to the time it takes for one walking step, and is worth practicing beforehand. You will find that any recorded music will have a regular walking beat, and that most of these can be divided into two, which is a good way to practice beforehand. A good time to experience the difference in movement is in during the creative movement, and it can also be demonstrated on percussion during free instrument play.

Space
Just like we prepare a suitable area for specific activities like painting, cooking or dancing, it is necessary to prepare a clear, unobstructed space for learning the foundations of music through movement. And just as we learn maths by adding and taking away concrete objects, so people learning music need to experience the concrete physical elements of space, time and energy, like the jogging quavers or jogging-quickly semiquavers.

Expectation
Each session begins and ends with the same Hello and Goodbye songs, indirectly preparing children for what will happen next. These non-verbal signals contribute enormously to behaviour, helping children to balance their emotions and manage their self-control independently. There are a few standard non-verbal signals used in practice, including 'can you make a circle' (GGEAGE), 'sit down' (GC), 'stand up' (CG) and 'find a good space' (CEGC), which can be played on a simple instrument, like a toy xylophone.

Tunes
Most songs use notes in the minor third, like the traditional ambulance 'nee-naw' sound. This is usually the first musical interval we naturally sing because it is the easiest (think: 'dad-dy!'), so we use it to teach singing. When we can match someone else singing it, we can sing in tune.

FRANCES S. TURNBULL

Nursery Week 1&2

Whispering Voice
Hello Song

What you will need:

Masking tape music spots for sitting places.
Instruments and equipment out of reach.
Cover distractions with fabric.

Welcome children to Musicaliti!
Shall we practise our whispering voices:
(whisper) Do you have your whispering voice?
Let's practise our speaking voices:
(speak aloud) Do you have your speaking voice?
What about your singing voice:
(sing) Do you have your singing voice?
I think we're ready to begin!

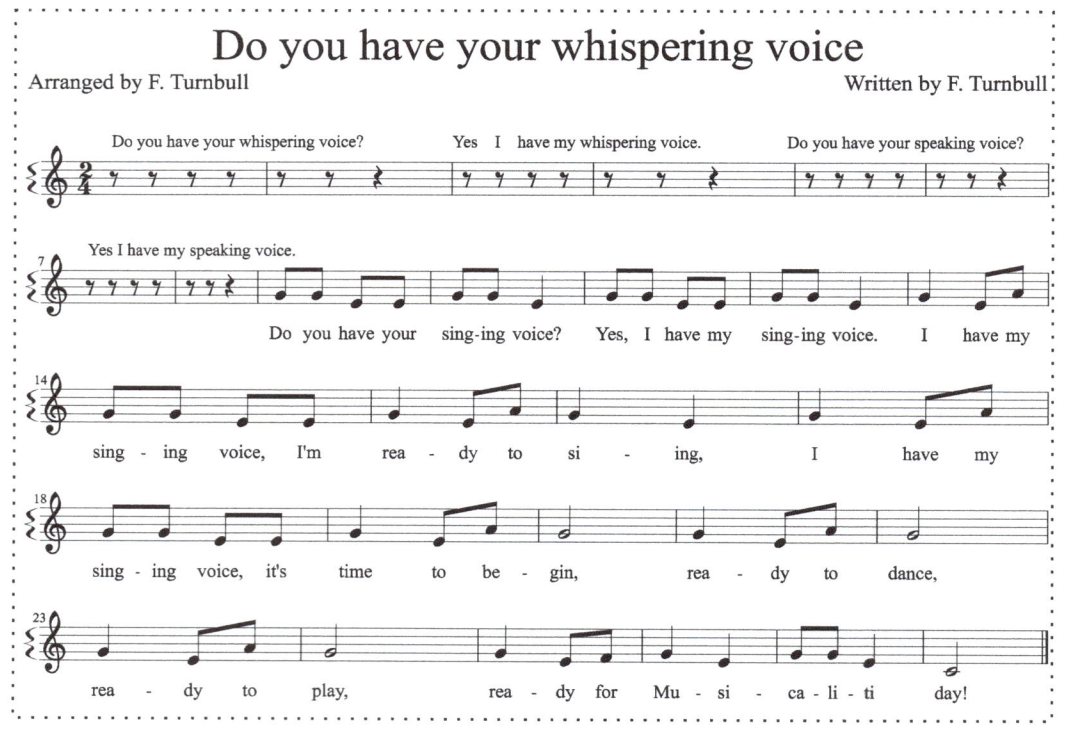

SPACE Statement

Social:
The welcoming greeting routine prepares children for a new activity as well as demonstrating a better way to start the day.

Physical:
Including whispering, speaking and singing allows children to experiment with communication.

Academic:
Developing sensitive listening helps children to respond better to instruction and detail.

Creative:
Teaching patterns develops children spatial planning and awareness.

Emotional:
Routine provides emotional security by knowing what to expect.

MAGICAL MUSICAL KINGDOM: NURSERY SERIES

Nursery Week 1&2

Old King Glory

Physical Warm Up

What you will need:

Week 1:   Tap knees
Week 2:   A scarf as a cloak for the 'King'

Focus: Walk to the crotchet beat.
Taking a step for every beat reinforces both the length of the crotchet as well as the continuous beat of music.

Today we're going to play a game
about a King called Old King Glory.
Sitting in a circle, we'll pretend to be a mountain
that Old King Glory walks around.
When you get tapped on the head,
it will be your turn to get up and follow Old King Glory.
Let's all tap our knees
as we sing about Old King Glory:
tap, tap, tap.

SPACE Statement

Social: The welcoming greeting routine prepares children for a new activity as well as demonstrating a better way to start the day.

Physical: Including whispering, speaking and singing allows children to experiment with communication.

Academic: Developing sensitive listening helps children to respond better to instruction and detail.

Creative: Teaching patterns develops children spatial planning and awareness.

Emotional: Routine provides emotional security by knowing what to expect.

Old King Glory
Arranged by F Turnbull — Traditional
Old King Glo-ry on the moun-tain, the moun-tain reached so high, it al-most touched the sky, and it's one, two, three, fol-low me.

FRANCES S. TURNBULL

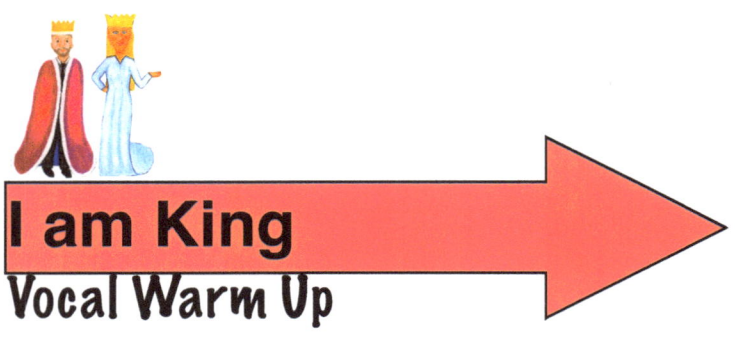

I am King
Vocal Warm Up

What you will need:

Week 1:   Drums
Week 2:   Scarves as capes

Focus: Tap a crotchet beat

This song uses the crotchet or quarter-note beat directly by having one word per beat. Every step, tap, shake or bang should be on every word. This song also uses notes in the minor third. This is the easiest musical interval to sing, and teaches the beginning of singing and matching tones.

Can you tap your drum? Listen to my drum.
Now let me listen to yours.
Kings don't walk quickly because they wear very heavy robes.
Can you pretend to go for a walk on your drum,
wearing a very heavy robe?
The King in our story is called King Crotchet.

**Nursery
Week 1 & 2**

SPACE Statement

Social: The welcoming greeting routine prepares children for a new activity as well as demonstrating a better way to start the day.

Physical: Including whispering, speaking and singing allows children to experiment with communication.

Academic: Developing sensitive listening helps children to respond better to instruction and detail.

Creative: Teaching patterns develops children spatial planning and awareness.

Emotional: Routine provides emotional security by knowing what to expect.

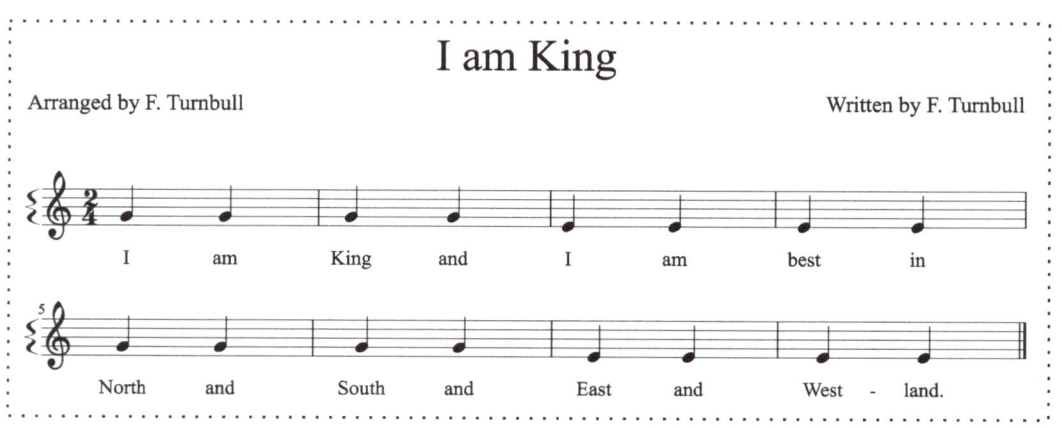

MAGICAL MUSICAL KINGDOM: NURSERY SERIES

Nursery Week 1&2

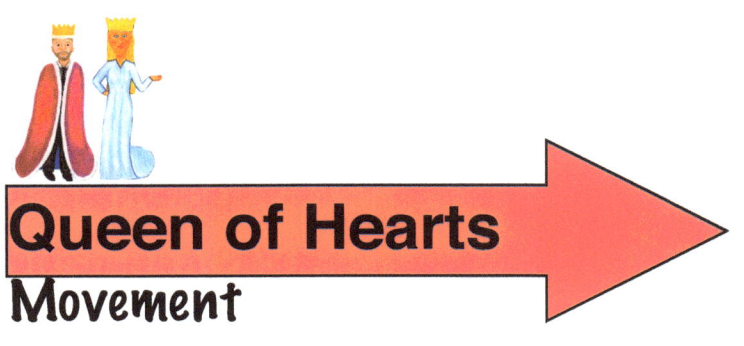

Queen of Hearts
Movement

What you will need:

Week 1 and 2: Stand in a circle and dance

Focus: Group circle dance as described.

Let's all stand up and hold hands in our circle.
Let's go around the circle this way and take eight steps:
one, two, three, four, five, six, seven, eight.
Now take four steps to the middle: one, two, three, four.
And take four steps back: one, two, three, four.
Let's go in a circle the other way, taking eight steps:
one, two, three, four, five, six, seven, eight.
Take four steps to the middle: one, two, three, four.
And four steps back: one, two, three, four.
I think we're ready to play our game!

SPACE Statement

Social: The welcoming greeting routine prepares children for a new activity as well as demonstrating a better way to start the day.

Physical: Including whispering, speaking and singing allows children to experiment with communication.

Academic: Developing sensitive listening helps children to respond better to instruction and detail.

Creative: Teaching patterns develops children spatial planning and awareness.

Emotional: Routine provides emotional security by knowing what to expect.

FRANCES S. TURNBULL

Nursery Week 1&2

Queen are Royal
Instrumental Play

What you will need:

Week 1 and 2:   Egg shakers

Focus: Jogging/shaking twice as quickly
Judge the group to decide whether to stick to shaking eggs and get them up and jogging in the second week.

Who know what the king's wife is called?
Yes, she is called the queen.
The queen in our story is called Queen Quaver.
She moves a bit quicker than King Crotchet, like she is jogging.
Can you use these egg shakers as if you are jogging?
Jog-jog-jog-jog-jog and stop.
Did you manage to stop your shakers?
Let's do it again. Jog-jog-jog-jog and stop.
Queen Quaver loves to tell everybody how the water shines and glistens in the Magical Musical Kingdom.
Let's get our egg shakers as we sing,
and you can even find different parts of your body to tap with your shakers!

SPACE Statement

Social: The welcoming greeting routine prepares children for a new activity as well as demonstrating a better way to start the day.

Physical: Including whispering, speaking and singing allows children to experiment with communication.

Academic: Developing sensitive listening helps children to respond better to instruction and detail.

Creative: Teaching patterns develops children spatial planning and awareness.

Emotional: Routine provides emotional security by knowing what to expect.

MAGICAL MUSICAL KINGDOM: NURSERY SERIES

Nursery Week 1&2

King & Queen
Story/Investigation

What you will need:

Week 1 and 2:   Pictures and characters

* Try out the character games using tennis balls and rolling them through children's legs (croquet); or sitting children in pairs and rolling a tennis ball back and forth (tennis).

Are you ready for a story?
It's quite exciting, and every week, we hear a bit more!
This is a picture of the Magical Musical Kingdom.
Let's rub our ears and get them ready to listen.

A long time ago in a Magical Musical Kingdom far, far away, there lived King Crotchet. King Crotchet was big and strong and when he walked past, everyone stopped to watch him because he was so loud and took such big steps. King Crotchet ruled wisely and justly and had a great crown full of every precious stone in the world. People loved King Crotchet so much that they travelled far and wide to find the most precious stone and every week, he would choose the best new precious stones to add to his crown. The rest of the precious stones were added to the walls of his magnificent castle that shone each morning on the magical hill. Every day King Crotchet loved to play croquet, a game where he would hit four balls though four hoops in the ground.

The Crotchet King was married to Queen Quaver. Queen Quaver moved quickly and quietly, and she was always two steps ahead of the King. Queen Quaver was very beautiful, the most beautiful lady in the land, and people travelled from all over the world to see her. Wherever she went, the mountains peaked higher, the grass shone greener, the flowers grew brighter and even the rivers shone until they glistened, although she hardly made a sound. Queen Quaver loved to play tennis and would always bounce and hit the ball as quickly as she could.

SPACE Statement

Social: The welcoming greeting routine prepares children for a new activity as well as demonstrating a better way to start the day.

Physical: Including whispering, speaking and singing allows children to experiment with communication.

Academic: Developing sensitive listening helps children to respond better to instruction and detail.

Creative: Teaching patterns develops children spatial planning and awareness.

Emotional: Routine provides emotional security by knowing what to expect.

Nursery Week 1&2

SPACE Statement

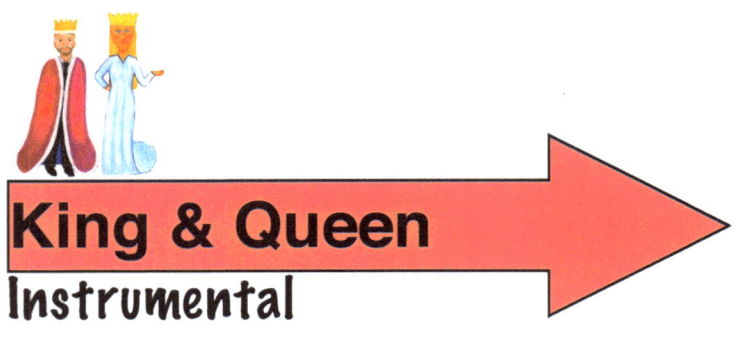

King & Queen
Instrumental

What you will need:

Week 1: None
Track length: 3.04 (Clear Air, K.McCleod)

This time is for creative expression without talking. Using body percussion, explore tapping the body (head, ears, shoulders, tummy, toes), claps and patches (knee taps), steps and stomps. Starting from head to toe helps in preventing repetition. The music is in **4/4** time, so tap in time to the music and only change to a new movement after a count of **4**.

Focus on contrasts like loud/quiet, high/low, fast/slow.

Week 2: None
Track length: 2.39 (Cattails, K. McCleod)

This time is for creative expression without talking. Move in time or play instruments to the tune that you hear. Beat is the regular timing of the song, while rhythm follows the song words or tune, so choose whether to play to the beat or the rhythm of the song.

Focus on contrasts like loud/quiet, high/low, fast/slow.

It's time to listen to music
and find a creative way to respond.
Be sure to listen to how the music sounds,
whether it is high or low, quick or slow,
and try to copy it.
Let's find lots of different ways
to respond to the music.

Social: The welcoming greeting routine prepares children for a new activity as well as demonstrating a better way to start the day.

Physical: Including whispering, speaking and singing allows children to experiment with communication.

Academic: Developing sensitive listening helps children to respond better to instruction and detail.

Creative: Teaching patterns develops children spatial planning and awareness.

Emotional: Routine provides emotional security by knowing what to expect.

MAGICAL MUSICAL KINGDOM: NURSERY SERIES

Nursery Week 1&2

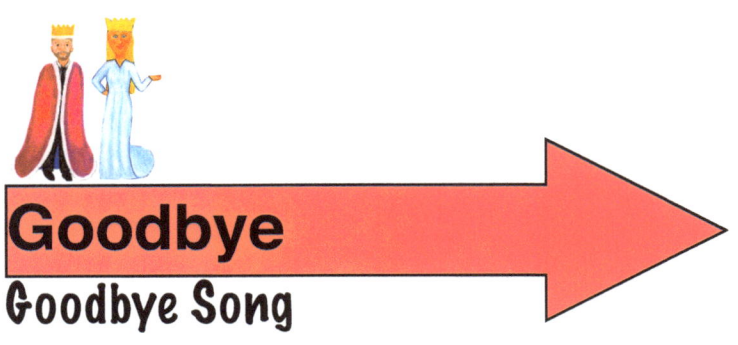

Goodbye

Goodbye Song

What you will need:

Week 1 and 2:   Sit in circle to sing goodbye.

The recording can be used when singing to younger children who won't sing back yet. Stop after "but now it's time to say" so that you can sing to each child, and wait for them to sing back their response. This is a perfect opportunity to determine whether children are singing in tune on their own.

If stickers have been used as rewards for behaviour during the session, this is also the time to ensure that each child receives a sticker, showing each child that you value them equally.

> What an exciting day we've had,
> playing Kings and Queens!
> It's time to go, so let's get our
> waving hands ready
> as we get ready to sing goodbye.

SPACE Statement

Social: The welcoming greeting routine prepares children for a new activity as well as demonstrating a better way to start the day.

Physical: Including whispering, speaking and singing allows children to experiment with communication.

Academic: Developing sensitive listening helps children to respond better to instruction and detail.

Creative: Teaching patterns develops children spatial planning and awareness.

Emotional: Routine provides emotional security by knowing what to expect.

Goodbye my Friends — Arranged by F. Turnbull, Written by F. Turnbull

Good-bye my friends, good-bye, we've had a love-ly day, we love to sing and dance and play, but now it's time to say: Good-bye (name) Good-bye (name) Good-bye (name) we've had a love-ly day.

FRANCES S. TURNBULL

Nursery Week 3&4

2 KNIGHT & LADY

Knight Quaver-Crotchet
This is the first rhythm that we teach and it sounds like three quick notes and a short rest, which matches the bass line of Queen's "We will, we will, rock you!". It uses the previous notes that we introduced (crotchet and quaver) and acts as a reminder of the literal difference between jogging and walking by experiencing a "jog-jog-walk" or stepping 'short-short-long'. This matches Knight Quaver-Crotchet's character, as he is a knight on a horse who gallops and slows, gallops and slows as he goes around protecting the kingdom. This is also an opportune moment to mention that in the Magical Musical Kingdom, we protect our friends and make sure that they do not get hurt, so in real life, we make sure that our eyes are watching where we are going, and where our arms and legs are moving to protect our real friends.

Lady Minim
In contrast to Queen Quaver, who moves twice as quickly as the King, Lady Minim moves twice as slowly as the King. Our story explains that Lady Minim is a friend to all the animals and she cannot move quickly or she would frighten them away. She looks after the animals whenever they are ill, so the children can pretend that they each have a small animal that they are stroking or carrying. Moving along with any recorded music can develop your awareness of taking one long step for every two beats that the King would walk. The important element here is that each note leads on to the next, that the steps are long and start as soon as the other ended, like slow motion walking.

Personal Space
Sitting in a circle for the hello and goodbye songs as well as during instrument play, ensures that everyone can be seen and acknowledged, everyone is 'at the front', and most importantly, children do not get left out or hidden by other children. When standing up, children have a natural tendency to stand together in groups until they are comfortable and secure in their own space. To encourage this, the instruction 'find a good space' can be used with a little tune: CEGC. In time, this tune can be played on a xylophone or other instrument without using words, as a signal or automatic reminder of what to do. Remind children to slowly stretch their arms out around them so that they are not touching, and to turn around slowly to make sure that they have enough room to move without touching others.

Instrument Play
Using identical instruments automatically ensures that there are no 'favourite' instruments, preventing disappointment. More than this, identical instruments allows children to find creative ways to use the instruments while also allowing children to imitate each other. To reduce the potential monotony of only shaking or tapping in one position, get children to tap on their toes/knees/tummy/shoulders etc. By deciding to start from shoulders to toes or vice versa, you create a logical sequence that doesn't necessarily need to be explained, yet is easy to follow and may even give you ideas of different body parts in between that might be more appropriate without the possibility of repeating the same parts.

MAGICAL MUSICAL KINGDOM: NURSERY SERIES

Nursery Week 1&2

Whispering Voice

Hello Song

What you will need:

Masking tape music spots for sitting places.
Instruments and equipment out of reach.
Cover distractions with fabric.

Welcome children to Musicaliti!
Shall we practise our whispering voices:
(whisper) Do you have your whispering voice?
Let's practise our speaking voices:
(speak aloud) Do you have your speaking voice?
What about your singing voice:
(sing) Do you have your singing voice?
I think we're ready to begin!

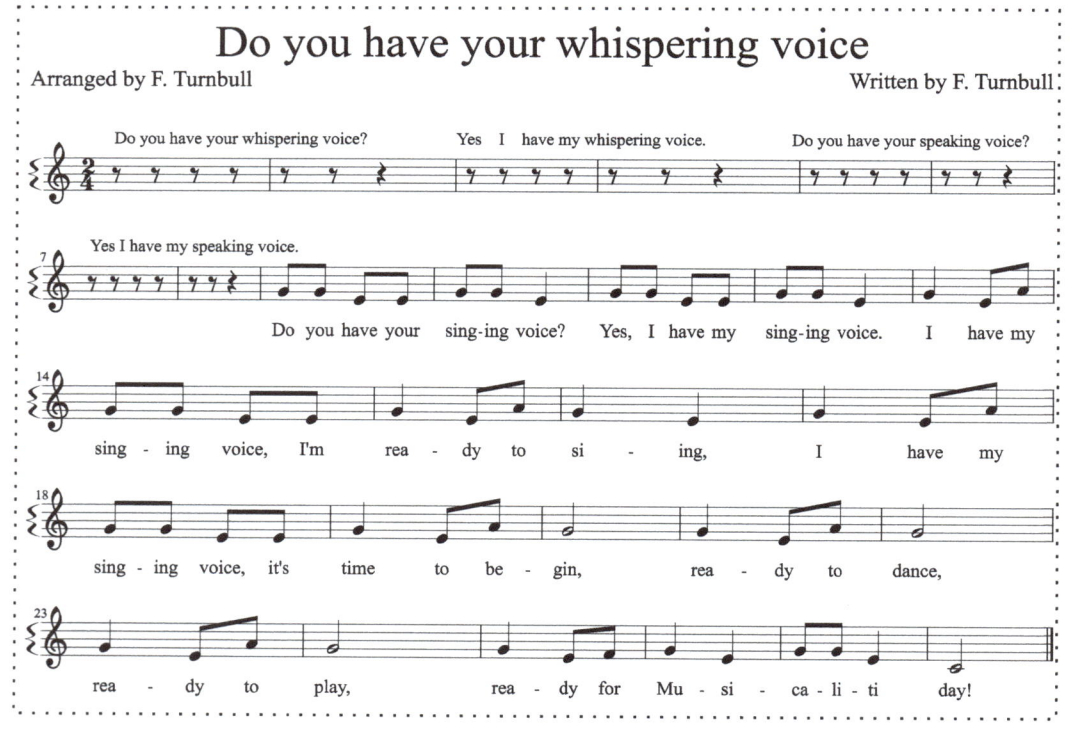

SPACE Statement

Social: The welcoming greeting routine prepares children for a new activity as well as demonstrating a better way to start the day.

Physical: Including whispering, speaking and singing allows children to experiment with communication.

Academic: Developing sensitive listening helps children to respond better to instruction and detail.

Creative: Teaching patterns develops children spatial planning and awareness.

Emotional: Routine provides emotional security by knowing what to expect.

Nursery Week 3&4

Knight & Horse
Physical Warm Up

What you will need:

Week 3 and 4:   Rhythm sticks

Focus: Keep a simple, repeated rhythm

Sing the song through and let the children repeat line for line, to the tune of 'We Will Rock You' by Queen. In the first week, gallop to the rhythm. In the second week, play the rhythm sticks to the rhythm.

Knights wore heavy armour and rode horses.
Let's practice moving around with heavy armour and swords.
Now pretend that you are the brave horse, gallop-a-gallop.
Are you looking where you are galloping?
Knights never crash into their friends but they protect them!.

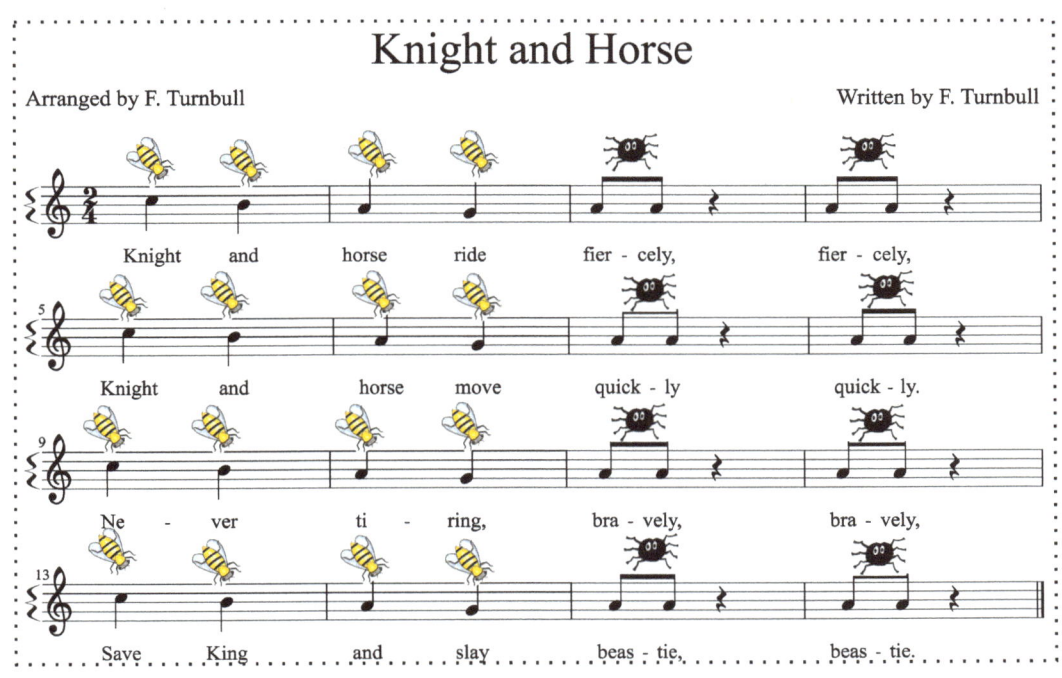

Knight and Horse
Arranged by F. Turnbull — Written by F. Turnbull

Knight and horse ride fier-cely, fier-cely,
Knight and horse move quick-ly, quick-ly.
Ne-ver ti-ring, bra-vely, bra-vely,
Save King and slay beas-tie, beas-tie.

SPACE Statement

Social: The welcoming greeting routine prepares children for a new activity as well as demonstrating a better way to start the day.

Physical: Including whispering, speaking and singing allows children to experiment with communication.

Academic: Developing sensitive listening helps children to respond better to instruction and detail.

Creative: Teaching patterns develops children spatial planning and awareness.

Emotional: Routine provides emotional security by knowing what to expect.

MAGICAL MUSICAL KINGDOM: NURSERY SERIES

Nursery
Week 3 & 4

Grand Old Duke
Vocal Warm Up

What you will need:

Week 3:   None
Week 4:   Shakers

Focus: Showing different levels
Levels teach reading notation. Young children manage 2 levels (up-down); older children 3 levels (up-middle-down).

Knight's friend may have been the Grand Old Duke of York.
I'm sure you know this one,
so let's tap or move as if we're marching.
Left, left, left, right, left, left, left, left, right, left.
Protect your kingdom by moving carefully around your friends.

SPACE Statement

Social: The welcoming greeting routine prepares children for a new activity as well as demonstrating a better way to start the day.

Physical: Including whispering, speaking and singing allows children to experiment with communication.

Academic: Developing sensitive listening helps children to respond better to instruction and detail.

Creative: Teaching patterns develops children spatial planning and awareness.

Emotional: Routine provides emotional security by knowing what to expect.

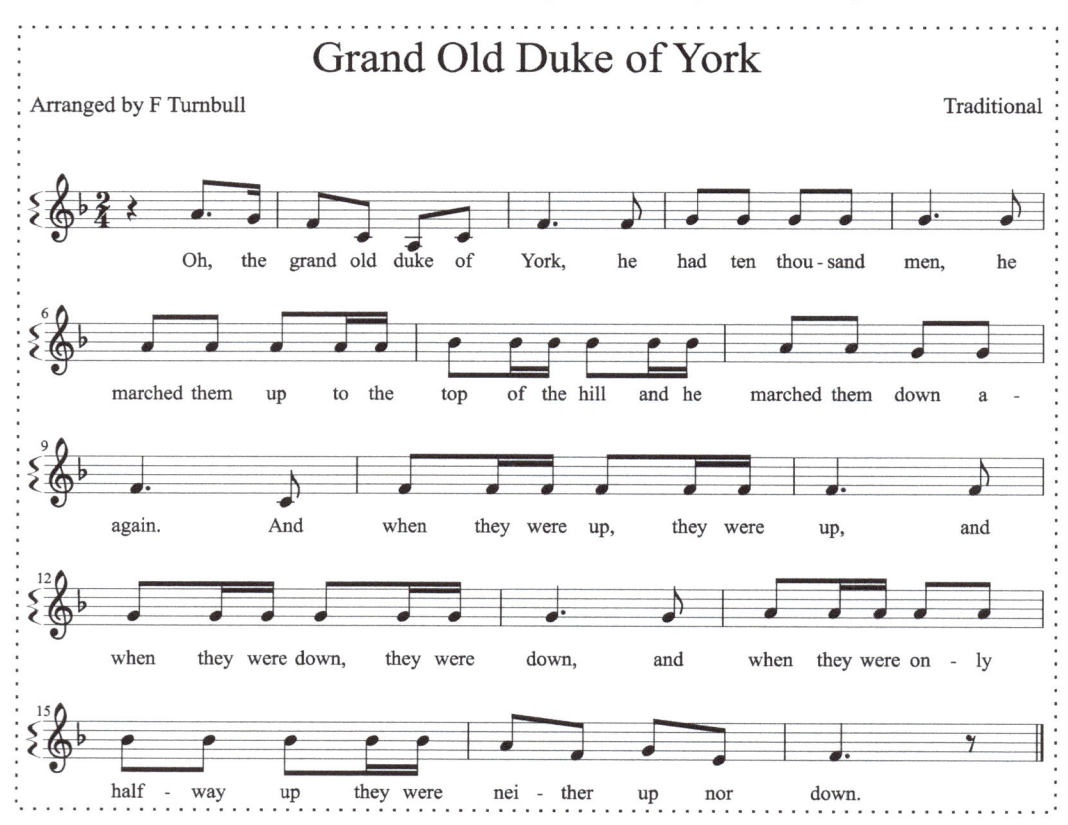

FRANCES S. TURNBULL

Nursery Week 3&4

Down came my friend

Instrument Play

What you will need:

Week 3 and 4:   Masking tape parallel lines

Focus: Group dancing in parallel lines

This game teaches children to move together in time and space. The pair opposite each other moves together to the end of the line and at their turn, walks or dances together down the middle of the line. This helps to explain concepts like harmonising.

Let's play the friend game!
Choose a music spot to stand opposite your friend.
The two friends at the end of the line have to take a wiggly walk
down the middle of the line.
When they get to the other end, they join the side lines
and the two new people at the other end have a turn
to walk down the middle doing a wiggly dance.
Let's sing it through once.
Fantastic! Now let's try it with the whole song.

SPACE Statement

Social: The welcoming greeting routine prepares children for a new activity as well as demonstrating a better way to start the day.

Physical: Including whispering, speaking and singing allows children to experiment with communication.

Academic: Developing sensitive listening helps children to respond better to instruction and detail.

Creative: Teaching patterns develops children spatial planning and awareness.

Emotional: Routine provides emotional security by knowing what to expect.

MAGICAL MUSICAL KINGDOM: NURSERY SERIES

Nursery Week 3&4

Pink Hat Lady

Movement

What you will need:

Week 3 and 4: Chime bar

Focus: Move twice as slowly as the King

In the first week, play the chime bar as you all walk around the room with the children walking slowly and pretending to stroke wounded animals. In the second week, sitting in a circle, pass the chime bar around to all the children, focusing on the length of the chime.

The Lady in our story wears all pink
and moves very slowly.
She was a friend to the animals and if they were hurt,
they would come to her because she was gentle.
Can you be gentle and pretend to stroke a small animal?
Which pretend animal are you stroking?
It may be a hedgehog, squirrel, bird or rabbit.
As we move slowly, pretend to stroke your animal,
moving slowly to the beat of the music.

SPACE Statement

Social: The welcoming greeting routine prepares children for a new activity as well as demonstrating a better way to start the day.

Physical: Including whispering, speaking and singing allows children to experiment with communication.

Academic: Developing sensitive listening helps children to respond better to instruction and detail.

Creative: Teaching patterns develops children spatial planning and awareness.

Emotional: Routine provides emotional security by knowing what to expect.

Pink Hat Lady
Arranged by F. Turnbull — Written by F. Turnbull

Pink hat, Pink shoes, posh frock, read news, nod and sip tea, lift hat, curt-sey.

Nursery Week 3&4

Knight & Lady
Story/investigation

What you will need:

Week 3 and 4:   Pictures and characters

Depending on time allowance and group, use the suggested activities for movement exploration.

Are you ready for a story?
It's quite exciting, and every week, we hear a bit more!
This is a picture of the Magical Musical Kingdom.
Let's rub our ears and get them ready to listen.

A long time ago in a Magical Musical Kingdom far away, there lived King Crochet married to Queen Quaver. They lived with a brave and handsome Knight Quaver-Crochet. He was the most brave person in all the land and would do anything to protect his King Crochet and Queen Quaver. When bad people took things from the King, Knight Quaver-Crochet would travel to the other side of the world and never give up until they were caught. He wasn't scared of anything or anyone because he was fit and well trained. When he was training, Knight Quaver-Crochet loved to fence, a sport with swords that relied on cunning and expertise.

Knight Quaver-Crochet was married to Lady Minim, a very special Lady who was very good at caring for sick animals. Lady Minim moved slowly and calmly so that they were never startled or afraid and some people said she could even speak the secret language of animals. When she wasn't caring for animals, Lady Minim loved to play bowls, gently rolling one ball to hit the bull's eye.

SPACE Statement

Social: The welcoming greeting routine prepares children for a new activity as well as demonstrating a better way to start the day.

Physical: Including whispering, speaking and singing allows children to experiment with communication.

Academic: Developing sensitive listening helps children to respond better to instruction and detail.

Creative: Teaching patterns develops children spatial planning and awareness.

Emotional: Routine provides emotional security by knowing what to expect.

MAGICAL MUSICAL KINGDOM: NURSERY SERIES

Nursery Week 3&4

Knight & Lady
Instrumental

What you will need:

Week 3:	None
Track length:	1.52 (Indended Force, K.McCleod)

This time is for creative expression without talking. Walk when the music starts slowly and clap as music gets quicker. Go back to walking as the music slows down. We are showing that the change in tempo (speed) changes the mood of the music: slow music is calm, fast music is intense.

Contrasting feet with hands is easier than fast/slow walking or clapping.

Week 4:	None
Track length:	2.55 (Relent, K. McCleod)

This time is for creative expression without talking. Demonstrate long steps, quick jogging, walking and stopping. Emphasize the different lengths of notation.

Focus on high/low contrasts by reaching up or down as appropriate.

It's time to listen to music
and find a creative way to respond.
Be sure to listen to how the music sounds,
whether it is high or low, quick or slow,
and try to copy it.
Let's find lots of different ways
to respond to the music.

SPACE Statement

Social: The welcoming greeting routine prepares children for a new activity as well as demonstrating a better way to start the day.

Physical: Including whispering, speaking and singing allows children to experiment with communication.

Academic: Developing sensitive listening helps children to respond better to instruction and detail.

Creative: Teaching patterns develops children spatial planning and awareness.

Emotional: Routine provides emotional security by knowing what to expect.

Nursery Week 3&4

Goodbye

Goodbye Song

What you will need:

Week 1 and 2:   Sit in circle to sing goodbye.

The recording can be used when singing to younger children who won't sing back yet. Stop after "but now it's time to say" so that you can sing to each child, and wait for them to sing back their response. This is a perfect opportunity to determine whether children are singing in tune on their own.

If stickers have been used as rewards for behaviour during the session, this is also the time to ensure that each child receives a sticker, showing each child that you value them equally.

> What an exciting day we've had,
> playing Kings and Queens!
> It's time to go, so let's get our
> waving hands ready
> as we get ready to sing goodbye.

SPACE Statement

Social: The welcoming greeting routine prepares children for a new activity as well as demonstrating a better way to start the day.

Physical: Including whispering, speaking and singing allows children to experiment with communication.

Academic: Developing sensitive listening helps children to respond better to instruction and detail.

Creative: Teaching patterns develops children spatial planning and awareness.

Emotional: Routine provides emotional security by knowing what to expect.

MAGICAL MUSICAL KINGDOM: NURSERY SERIES

Nursery Week 5&6

3 PRINCESS & PRINCE

Princess Semiquaver
Princess Semiquaver is the quickest beat that we do at this level: four quick beats to the value of one King Crotchet step. While the pace suggests a non-specific, quick run to the children, the true rhythm is to take four quick steps for every beat of the pulse (ongoing beat), and the children's accuracy of this is left to your discretion, taking into account the age and abilities of your group. In our story, Princess Semiquaver is a young princess who loves playing by a river, and happened to befriend a little frog that had a green body and yellow head. Everyday he performed little tricks and somersaults, told jokes and made the princess laugh, and one day, she laughed so much that she kissed him, which turned him back into a Prince.

Frog Prince
Frog Prince is a Prince with a horse, and he was turned into a frog by a naughty Goblin. His horse's movement is the rhythm of this session, as the semi-quaver-dotted-quaver rhythm shows that this is a gallop: quick-slow, quick-slow, quick-slow. This is best demonstrated keeping one foot in front of the other and galloping around the room using your back leg first, much like a child learning to skip. This is different to skipping in that skipping (Flying Fairy) has the notation the other way around (slow-quick), giving the body time to gain momentum to move forward on the first step, while the short second note shows that the same leg is used twice, and then swaps to the other side.

Circle Games
Shapes can be explored in many ways, and the concrete experience of circle games helps a number of areas of development, including numeracy. Walking around in a circle develops the abstract ability of following an imaginary line, while holding hands develops the social awareness of not holding hands too tightly while keeping a comfortable distance apart. Circle games also develop spatial awareness, as most circle games at some point involve leaving a set point and returning back to it: a place that only really exists in our imagination, even if moving forward and then back out. This song is a useful addition to your circle game repertoire beyond Ring a Rosies and Farmer in the Dell.

Directional Movement
When given the freedom to move around a room, whether walking, jogging, running, galloping, skipping and any other movement, possibly because it is expected, people generally automatically follow a circular pathway. It is useful to get children to not only start movement sessions by 'finding a good space', but to also **keep** their own space while moving because this helps them to explore and express their individuality. Practically, this means that children should be encouraged to move in different directions around the room whilst being aware of others. Move into empty areas, usually corners, and even change direction as they move, walking backwards, sideways or diagonally. During the activity, praise children who 'get it', allowing others to imitate them, as this reassures the group and reaffirms what is expected, but never stop an activity when children are trying to get it right.

FRANCES S. TURNBULL

Nursery Week 5&6

Whispering Voice

Hello Song

What you will need:

Masking tape music spots for sitting places.
Instruments and equipment out of reach.
Cover distractions with fabric.

Welcome children to Musicaliti!
Shall we practise our whispering voices:
(whisper) Do you have your whispering voice?
Let's practise our speaking voices:
(speak aloud) Do you have your speaking voice?
What about your singing voice:
(sing) Do you have your singing voice?
I think we're ready to begin!

SPACE Statement

Social: The welcoming greeting routine prepares children for a new activity as well as demonstrating a better way to start the day.

Physical: Including whispering, speaking and singing allows children to experiment with communication.

Academic: Developing sensitive listening helps children to respond better to instruction and detail.

Creative: Teaching patterns develops children spatial planning and awareness.

Emotional: Routine provides emotional security by knowing what to expect.

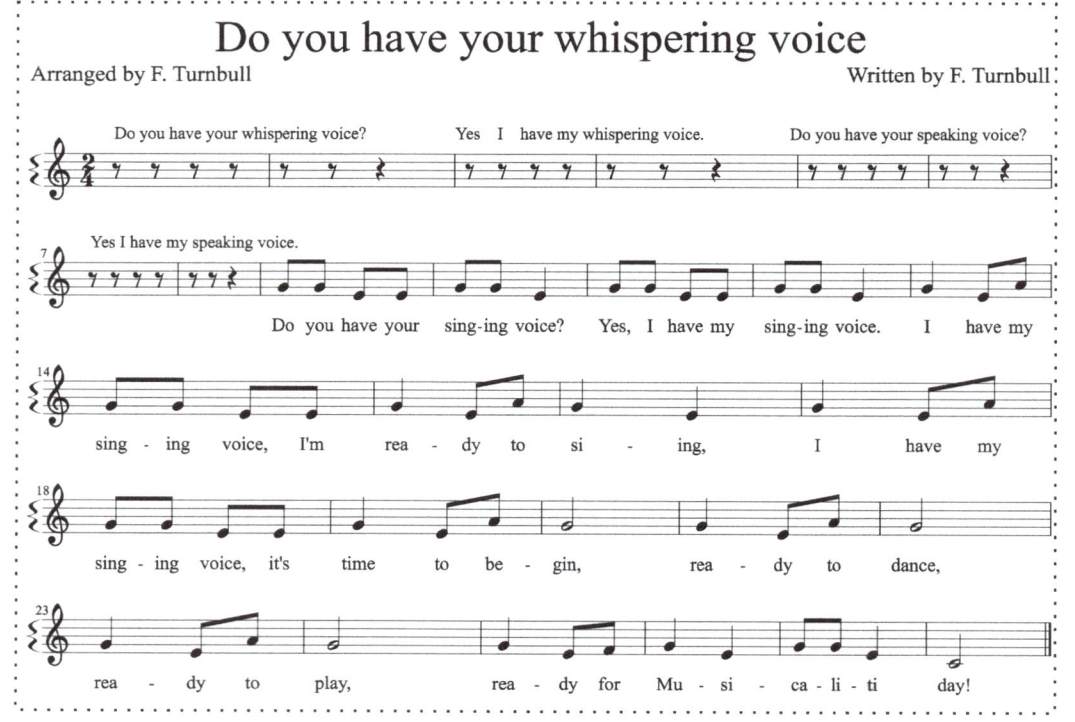

MAGICAL MUSICAL KINGDOM: NURSERY SERIES

Nursery Week 5 & 6

Semiquaver
Physical Warm Up

What you will need:

Week 5 and 6:   Group dancing, masking tape spots

V2:   Circle to the right, semiquaver, Circle to the right, semiquaver,
      Circle to the right, semiquaver, You're the one my darling ("crouch down")
V3:   Everybody up, semiquaver, Everybody down, semiquaver
      Everybody up, semiquaver, You're the one my darling ("to the middle")
V4:   Everybody in, semiquaver, Everybody out, semiquaver
      Everybody in, semiquaver, You're the one my darling!

It's time to play a Princess game.
Let's hold hands while standing on our music spot.
Let's walk around the circle to the left: one, two, ready, stop.
Now let's walk to the right: one, two, ready, stop.
Can you crouch down? Let's jump up! And back down. Now up! Can you walk forward slowly? One, two, ready, stop.
And now backwards: one, two, ready, stop.
I think we're ready to play our Princess game!

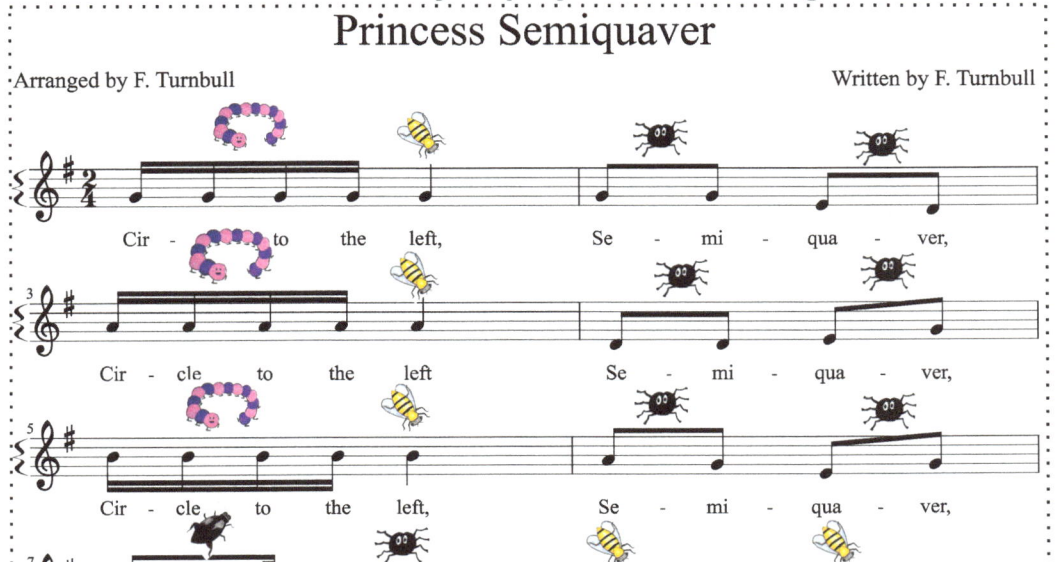

SPACE Statement

Social: The welcoming greeting routine prepares children for a new activity as well as demonstrating a better way to start the day.

Physical: Including whispering, speaking and singing allows children to experiment with communication.

Academic: Developing sensitive listening helps children to respond better to instruction and detail.

Creative: Teaching patterns develops children spatial planning and awareness.

Emotional: Routine provides emotional security by knowing what to expect.

FRANCES S. TURNBULL

Nursery Week 5&6

Built my Princess
Vocal Warm Up

What you will need:

Week 5:   None
Week 6:   Sandblocks

Focus: Clapping in pairs

Demonstrate holding hands up ready for a clapping game, and then, clapping together in pairs.

Use sandblocks the second week doing the same activity.

Can you pretend to build a house for our princess?
We could pretend to pass each other bricks
by playing a clapping game.
Can you find a partner and clap your hands on theirs?
Clap, clap, clap and stop.
Oh dear, I think the princess has jumped out!
Can you wave goodbye to your friend and find another partner?
Let's build our house with our new partner:
Clap, clap, clap and stop.
Now, wave goodbye to your partner, and find a new one.
I think we're ready to play this game with the song!

SPACE Statement

Social: The welcoming greeting routine prepares children for a new activity as well as demonstrating a better way to start the day.

Physical: Including whispering, speaking and singing allows children to experiment with communication.

Academic: Developing sensitive listening helps children to respond better to instruction and detail.

Creative: Teaching patterns develops children spatial planning and awareness.

Emotional: Routine provides emotional security by knowing what to expect.

MAGICAL MUSICAL KINGDOM: NURSERY SERIES

Nursery Week 5&6

Hopping, Hopping

Movement

What you will need:

Week 5 and 6:   None

Focus: Drama, acting out frog jumps.

All hop around the room (crouch, jump) until the last line and all blow kisses ('kiss, kiss, kiss'), then stand up tall ('now I am a prince').

In week 6, half the children can be frogs and the rest, princes, and then swap over.

A long time ago, a naughty Goblin turned a Prince into a frog!
The frog-prince had to live by the river, and oneday
Princess Semiquaver came to play with him.
He always told her funny jokes and did clever tricks.
Can you do a clever trick?
One day he told the Princess a really funny joke and trick
and she laughed and laughed, and then gave him a kiss.
Boom! Suddenly he turned into a Prince!
Let's hop around like frogs as we sing a hopping song!
Then we can blow kisses as we get ready to turn into a prince
by standing up and pretending to put on a crown.

SPACE Statement

Social: The welcoming greeting routine prepares children for a new activity as well as demonstrating a better way to start the day.

Physical: Including whispering, speaking and singing allows children to experiment with communication.

Academic: Developing sensitive listening helps children to respond better to instruction and detail.

Creative: Teaching patterns develops children spatial planning and awareness.

Emotional: Routine provides emotional security by knowing what to expect.

Hopping Hopping
Arranged by F. Turnbull — Written by F. Turnbull

Hop-ping hop-ping on a log, I'm a hop-ping lit-tle frog.
Kiss, kiss, kiss, now I am a prince!

Nursery Week 5&6

Litte Bells
Instrumental Play

What you will need:

Week 5 and 6: Bells

Focus: Jingle bells while singing solo

In week 2, pass one bell around the group, with each child singing on their own when they have the bell. The rest of the group can tap their knees until it is their turn. Demonstrate the last 5 notes for the group beforehand as it can be tricky: ding, dong, ding, dong-dong.

The Prince originally came from Westminster,
far, far away from the Magical Musical Kingdom.
In Westminster there are loads of bells,
so Frog-Prince sang a song to Princess Semiquaver.
Can you copy me: ding, dong, ding-dong-dong.
Let's jingle our bells and then pass them to
our friend next to us on our left.

SPACE Statement

Social: The welcoming greeting routine prepares children for a new activity as well as demonstrating a better way to start the day.

Physical: Including whispering, speaking and singing allows children to experiment with communication.

Academic: Developing sensitive listening helps children to respond better to instruction and detail.

Creative: Teaching patterns develops children spatial planning and awareness.

Emotional: Routine provides emotional security by knowing what to expect.

The Little Bells — Arranged by F Turnbull — Traditional

MAGICAL MUSICAL KINGDOM: NURSERY SERIES

Nursery Week 5&6

Princess & Prince

Story/Investigation

What you will need:

Week 5 and 6:   Pictures and characters

Depending on time allowance and group, use the suggested activities for movement exploration.

Are you ready for a story?
It's quite exciting, and every week, we hear a bit more!
This is a picture of the Magical Musical Kingdom.
Let's rub our ears and get them ready to listen.

A long time ago in a Magical Musical Kingdom far away, there lived King Crochet married to Queen Quaver, protected by the brave and handsome Knight Quaver-Crochet who was married to Lady Minim who looked after the animals. In this household lived the King's most precious jewel, his daughter, Princess Semiquaver. Semiquaver moved even more quickly than the Queen and was often running quickly or spinning in fields, forests and near ponds with all the animals of the Kingdom. Starting very quietly she got louder and louder as she got further away from the Castle. One day when she was at the pond, she saw a little frog. He had a beautiful golden head and she thought he looked like a little prince so she called him Frog Prince.

Princess Semiquaver always visited Frog Prince with a juicy bug and one day, Frog Prince did a froggy somersault trick and told a funny joke. She laughed out loud, and thought he was so clever that she gave him a kiss. Poof! Suddenly he disappeared and a handsome prince appeared in his place, from a spell that a naughty Goblin put on him. He loved his new name so much that he was known by everyone as Frog Prince. He used to croak very loudly and was so glad that now he could speak quietly, too. His favourite sport was horse riding and now that he was a person again, Frog Prince could ride his horse.

SPACE Statement

Social: The welcoming greeting routine prepares children for a new activity as well as demonstrating a better way to start the day.

Physical: Including whispering, speaking and singing allows children to experiment with communication.

Academic: Developing sensitive listening helps children to respond better to instruction and detail.

Creative: Teaching patterns develops children spatial planning and awareness.

Emotional: Routine provides emotional security by knowing what to expect.

Princess & Prince

Instrumental

What you will need:

Week 5: None
Track length: 1.58 (Electrodoodle, K.McCleod)

This time is for creative expression without talking. Demonstrate different ways to enjoy music without running or moving in a circle. Find different ways to express building up to the crescendo in the second part. Through freedance, we allow children to explore their own individual movement signature without imposing our own sense or style on them.

Listen for loud/quiet, high/low, fast/slow sounds and express them.

Week 6: None
Track length: 1.20 (Divertissement, K. McCleod)

This time is for creative expression without talking. Demonstrate responding to a change in key by starting with skipping, then clapping and knee-tapping when the music changes, then back to skipping.

Listen for pauses and clearly respond to them.

Nursery Week 5&6

SPACE Statement

Social: The welcoming greeting routine prepares children for a new activity as well as demonstrating a better way to start the day.

Physical: Including whispering, speaking and singing allows children to experiment with communication.

Academic: Developing sensitive listening helps children to respond better to instruction and detail.

Creative: Teaching patterns develops children spatial planning and awareness.

Emotional: Routine provides emotional security by knowing what to expect.

It's time to listen to music
and find a creative way to respond.
Be sure to listen to how the music sounds,
whether it is high or low, quick or slow,
and try to copy it.
Let's find lots of different ways
to respond to the music.

MAGICAL MUSICAL KINGDOM: NURSERY SERIES

Nursery Week 5 & 6

Goodbye

Goodbye Song

What you will need:

Week 1 and 2:	Sit in circle to sing goodbye.

The recording can be used when singing to younger children who won't sing back yet. Stop after "but now it's time to say" so that you can sing to each child, and wait for them to sing back their response. This is a perfect opportunity to determine whether children are singing in tune on their own.

If stickers have been used as rewards for behaviour during the session, this is also the time to ensure that each child receives a sticker, showing each child that you value them equally.

> What an exciting day we've had,
> playing Kings and Queens!
> It's time to go, so let's get our
> waving hands ready
> as we get ready to sing goodbye.

SPACE Statement

Social: The welcoming greeting routine prepares children for a new activity as well as demonstrating a better way to start the day.

Physical: Including whispering, speaking and singing allows children to experiment with communication.

Academic: Developing sensitive listening helps children to respond better to instruction and detail.

Creative: Teaching patterns develops children spatial planning and awareness.

Emotional: Routine provides emotional security by knowing what to expect.

FRANCES S. TURNBULL

Nursery Week 7&8

4 GOBLIN AND FAIRY

Goblin
Goblin introduces a limping rhythm, giving children the opportunity to experience the different lengths of the crotchet and quaver and creating a 'slow-quick-quick' or 'walk-jog-jog' sound, meaning that each syllable in the 'Goblin' song needs a step and a jog-jog. Goblin is a naughty green character who lives in a cave far away from the castle because he hates music. His cave is full of old musical instruments that he stole and broke, and hidden away, he also has a secret pot of gold. Goblin was very cross that Princess Semiquaver had changed the Frog Prince back into a Prince, so one night, he crept into the castle and stole the King's precious jewels and hid them in a tower, so Knight Quaver-Crotchet had to go on a quest to find them.

Flying Fairy
Flying Fairy skips and flies over the woods, and loves music so much that she cannot speak, only sing. This dotted-quaver-semi-quaver rhythm is just like skipping and flying, light and carefree, in contrast to the heavy, unbalanced feel of the slow-quick-quick, limping Goblin. Children who struggle to skip need the activity broken down to hopping on one foot and then the other, first in 8 counts, then four, then two, which is when you can introduce travelling between hops. This is a useful exercise in any group towards strengthening leg muscles. In our story, Flying Fairy hears about the stolen jewels and flies to Goblin's cave, where she takes his gold and hangs it on a moonbeam as punishment.

6/8 Swing Time
Most of the songs this time are written in 6/8 time, with the same feel as 'Row, Row, Row Your Boat' and 'Girls and Boys go out to Play', and the same forward/back or left/right feel. As it is in compound time, it has three beats per sway, which is what creates the time needed to swing each side, and it is useful to remind the children of the feel of it by leaning left and right, or balancing on one foot and then the other, like a pendulum. Well-known children's songs in this metre/time signature (6/8) include Pat-a-Cake, Wheels on the Bus, Rock a Bye Baby, Hickory Dickory Dock, and London Bridge.

Scarves
Scarves are the most resourceful instrument in any musical repertoire, ideally sheer and no bigger than 3 ft or 1 m square, with edges sewn closed and easy to wash. Curl them into your hand and let them spring out like a jack in the box; fold them carefully and lie down on a comfy pillow; wrap them around your head as a fancy headdress; use them as a King's cape, animal's tail or a bride's train; be the wind blowing or the rain pouring; be a ghost or a baby; or, like our story, use a scarf as the pot of gold that Flying Fairy took to hang on the moonbeam.

MAGICAL MUSICAL KINGDOM: NURSERY SERIES

Nursery Week 7&8

Whispering Voice

Hello Song

What you will need:

Masking tape music spots for sitting places.
Instruments and equipment out of reach.
Cover distractions with fabric.

Welcome children to Musicaliti!
Shall we practise our whispering voices:
(whisper) Do you have your whispering voice?
Let's practise our speaking voices:
(speak aloud) Do you have your speaking voice?
What about your singing voice:
(sing) Do you have your singing voice?
I think we're ready to begin!

SPACE Statement

Social: The welcoming greeting routine prepares children for a new activity as well as demonstrating a better way to start the day.

Physical: Including whispering, speaking and singing allows children to experiment with communication.

Academic: Developing sensitive listening helps children to respond better to instruction and detail.

Creative: Teaching patterns develops children spatial planning and awareness.

Emotional: Routine provides emotional security by knowing what to expect.

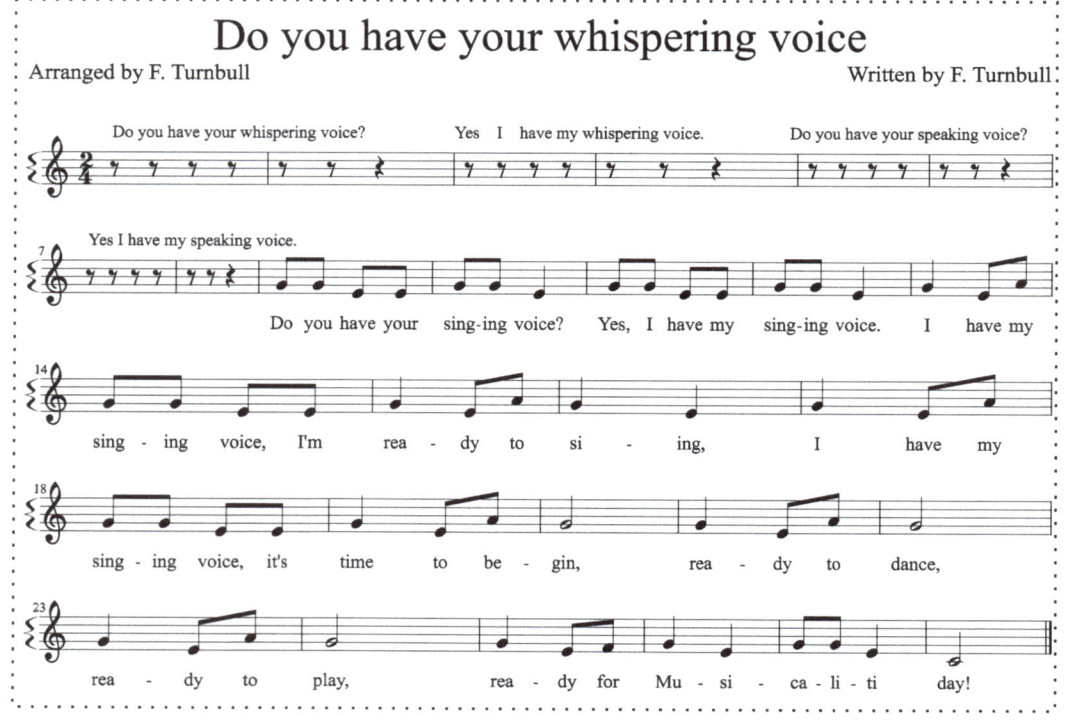

Do you have your whispering voice
Arranged by F. Turnbull — Written by F. Turnbull

Nursery Week 7 & 8

Goblin
Physical Warm Up

What you will need:

Week 7 and 8:   Egg shakers

Focus: Walking quietly to the 6/8 'swing'
This is the same feel as 'Row, row, row your boat', so demonstrate and encourage children to step to the 'swing' of the beat.

**This week our song is about the naughty Goblin
who stole the King's jewels.
He had a hunched back and limped.
Can you pretend to have a hunched back and limp?
He crept quietly because he only went out at night.
Can you creep quietly?
Then he carefully stole the King's jewels and hid them.
Can you pretend this egg shaker is a jewel
and find a place to hide it?
Let's stand up and creep like a naughty Goblin.**

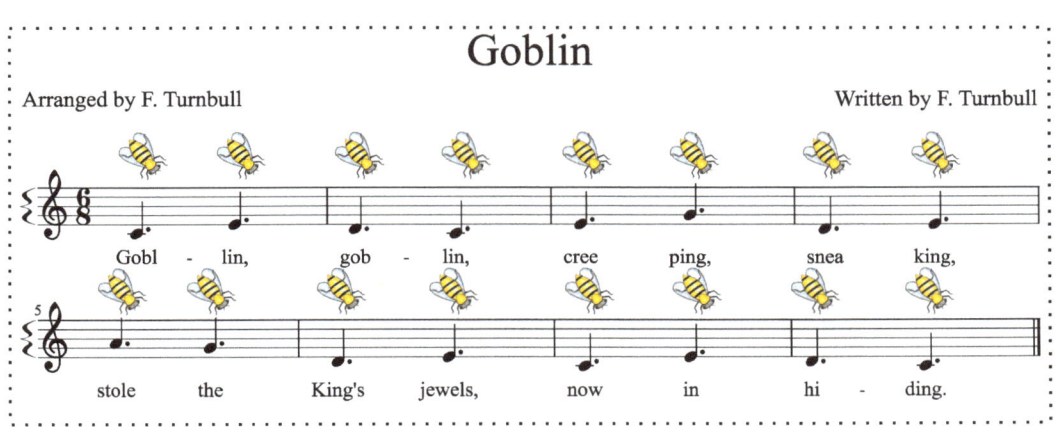

SPACE Statement

Social: The welcoming greeting routine prepares children for a new activity as well as demonstrating a better way to start the day.

Physical: Including whispering, speaking and singing allows children to experiment with communication.

Academic: Developing sensitive listening helps children to respond better to instruction and detail.

Creative: Teaching patterns develops children spatial planning and awareness.

Emotional: Routine provides emotional security by knowing what to expect.

MAGICAL MUSICAL KINGDOM: NURSERY SERIES

Nursery Week 7 & 8

Goblin Protector

Vocal Warm Up

What you will need:

Week 7 and 8:   Bells

Focus: Tap instruments on body parts.
Follow a logical sequence like toes, knees, tummy, elbows, shoulders, cheeks.

Our next game is about what happened to the naughty Goblin when the King and Queen found that the jewels were gone. Do you think the King and Queen would have been happy or cross? I think they would have been very cross.
Let's find different places to tap our instruments as we sing our song about the Green Goblin being sent to the Queen, but she didn't like him. Then he went to the King. But the King didn't like him, either, so he was sent back again. Are you ready for your instrument?

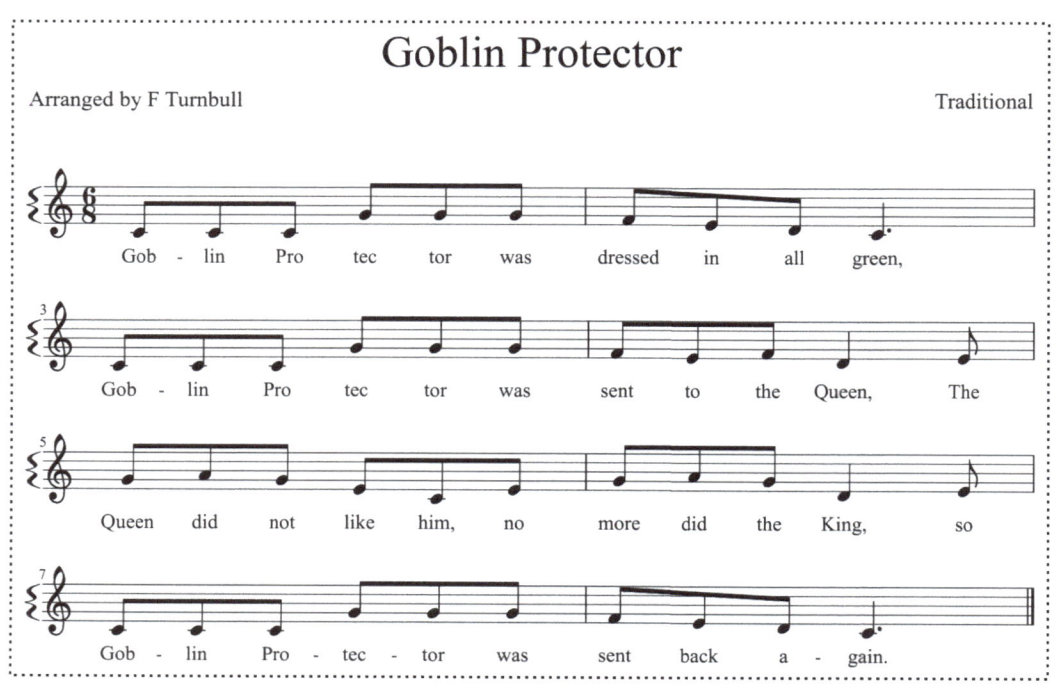

SPACE Statement

Social: The welcoming greeting routine prepares children for a new activity as well as demonstrating a better way to start the day.

Physical: Including whispering, speaking and singing allows children to experiment with communication.

Academic: Developing sensitive listening helps children to respond better to instruction and detail.

Creative: Teaching patterns develops children spatial planning and awareness.

Emotional: Routine provides emotional security by knowing what to expect.

Nursery Week 7&8

Flying Fairy
Movement

What you will need:

Week 7 and 8: Scarves (yellow for gold)

Focus: Free dance with scarves

The dance ends with children hanging scarves 'on a moonbeam', which may be your arm or another object.

Flying Fairy also lived in the Magical Musical Kingdom and she always sang when she spoke because she loved music.
Oneday as she skipped and flew over the woods, she heard about what the Green Goblin had done.
She got very cross and decided to take the Goblin's gold away and hang it high up on a moon beam.
Let's skip and fly around the room with these scarves, and pretend that they are the Goblin's gold.
Shall we hang it here? Let's get ready to fly!

Skipping Flying Fairy — Arranged by F. Turnbull, Written by F. Turnbull

Lyrics: Skipping, flying over the woods, / Elfen's gold, he's up to no good, / Skipping, flying way up high, / Hang gold on a moonbeam high.

SPACE Statement

Social: The welcoming greeting routine prepares children for a new activity as well as demonstrating a better way to start the day.

Physical: Including whispering, speaking and singing allows children to experiment with communication.

Academic: Developing sensitive listening helps children to respond better to instruction and detail.

Creative: Teaching patterns develops children spatial planning and awareness.

Emotional: Routine provides emotional security by knowing what to expect.

MAGICAL MUSICAL KINGDOM: NURSERY SERIES

Nursery Week 7&8

Love Somebody
Instrumental Play

What you will need:

Week 7 and 8:   Two types of shakers

Focus: Instrument pass around.
Be clear on which direction instruments will be passed and received.

We're going to play Flying Fairy's favourite game called Shaker Pass-Around.
Everybody starts with a different shaker and after we sing and shake,
we pass it on to the person next to us and get a new shaker.
When our song says '*love somebody but I won't say who*', find somewhere to hide your instrument, maybe under our jumper, behind our back, or up our trouser leg!
Then when our song says, '*love somebody and it's you, you, you*', pass it to your friend. Are you ready?

SPACE Statement

Social: The welcoming greeting routine prepares children for a new activity as well as demonstrating a better way to start the day.

Physical: Including whispering, speaking and singing allows children to experiment with communication.

Academic: Developing sensitive listening helps children to respond better to instruction and detail.

Creative: Teaching patterns develops children spatial planning and awareness.

Emotional: Routine provides emotional security by knowing what to expect.

Nursery Week 7&8

Goblin & Fairy
Story/Investigation

What you will need:

Week 7 and 8:   Pictures and characters
Depending on time allowance and group, use the suggested activities for movement exploration.

Are you ready for a story?
It's quite exciting, and every week, we hear a bit more!
This is a picture of the Magical Musical Kingdom.
Let's rub our ears and get them ready to listen.

A long time ago in a Magical Musical Kingdom far away, there lived King Crotchet married to Queen Quaver, protected by the brave and handsome Knight Quaver-Crotchet who was married to Lady Minim who looked after the animals and lived together with Princess Semiquaver and Frog Prince. But far away from the Magical Kingdom, in a dark and dreary cave full of broken instruments lived Green Goblin, the naughty, creeping goblin who turned Frog Prince into a frog. He didn't like musical instruments, only the sound of voices and when he was cross he crept around and broke all the instruments he could find. He was very cross with Princess Semiquaver for changing the Prince back so he did another magic spell and crept into the castle and stole the King's Jewels, taking them to a secret tower, far away from the castle. Everybody was very sad and King Crochet and Frog Prince were furious. Queen Quaver and Lady Minim asked Knight Quaver-Crotchet to please find them so Knight Quaver-Crochet left immediately to search every tower in the land to find the hidden jewels. While Knight Quaver-Crochet was searching every tower in the land, he came across Flying Fairy, who flew everywhere. He searched her tower, but the jewels just were not there. When he told Flying Fairy what Goblin had done and how sad Frog Prince was, Flying Fairy got very cross indeed. She never spoke, but played music because she was surrounded by every instrument in the world. She wanted to play a trick on Goblin so using her special magic, she flew to his dark cave and saw all the broken instruments. Right at the back of the cave was a very shiny pot of gold, hidden behind a tree stump. Flying Fairy picked it up and flew right to the moon and hung it on a moon beam as punishment!

SPACE Statement

Social: The welcoming greeting routine prepares children for a new activity as well as demonstrating a better way to start the day.

Physical: Including whispering, speaking and singing allows children to experiment with communication.

Academic: Developing sensitive listening helps children to respond better to instruction and detail.

Creative: Teaching patterns develops children spatial planning and awareness.

Emotional: Routine provides emotional security by knowing what to expect.

MAGICAL MUSICAL KINGDOM: NURSERY SERIES

Nursery Week 7&8

Goblin & Fairy
Instrumental

What you will need:

Week 7: None
Track length: 0.55 (Music to Delight, K.McCleod)

This time is for creative expression without talking. Play the body using a variety of taps, claps, steps and stomps.

The music is in 4/4 time so tap in time to the music and only change to tapping in a new position after a count of 4.

Contrast loud/quiet, high/low, fast/slow sounds and express them.

Week 8: None
Track length: 0.48 (Poofy Reel, K. McCleod)

This time is for creative expression without talking. Tap to the rhythm of the tune, or another simple rhythm, e.g. tap-tap-tap, tap-tap-tap.

The rhythm is the tune that the song follows (usually lyrics), and may be quicker or slower than the beat or pulse (constant beat).

It's time to listen to music
and find a creative way to respond.
Be sure to listen to how the music sounds,
whether it is high or low, quick or slow,
and try to copy it.
Let's find lots of different ways
to respond to the music.

SPACE Statement

Social: The welcoming greeting routine prepares children for a new activity as well as demonstrating a better way to start the day.

Physical: Including whispering, speaking and singing allows children to experiment with communication.

Academic: Developing sensitive listening helps children to respond better to instruction and detail.

Creative: Teaching patterns develops children spatial planning and awareness.

Emotional: Routine provides emotional security by knowing what to expect.

FRANCES S. TURNBULL

Nursery Week 7&8

Goodbye

Goodbye Song

What you will need:

Week 1 and 2:   Sit in circle to sing goodbye.

The recording can be used when singing to younger children who won't sing back yet. Stop after "but now it's time to say" so that you can sing to each child, and wait for them to sing back their response. This is a perfect opportunity to determine whether children are singing in tune on their own.

If stickers have been used as rewards for behaviour during the session, this is also the time to ensure that each child receives a sticker, showing each child that you value them equally.

> What an exciting day we've had,
> playing Kings and Queens!
> It's time to go, so let's get our
> waving hands ready
> as we get ready to sing goodbye.

SPACE Statement

Social: The welcoming greeting routine prepares children for a new activity as well as demonstrating a better way to start the day.

Physical: Including whispering, speaking and singing allows children to experiment with communication.

Academic: Developing sensitive listening helps children to respond better to instruction and detail.

Creative: Teaching patterns develops children spatial planning and awareness.

Emotional: Routine provides emotional security by knowing what to expect.

MAGICAL MUSICAL KINGDOM: NURSERY SERIES

Nursery Week 9 & 10

5 DRAGON & UNICORN

Dragon
Dragon Semibreve is the slowest of all the notes. Taking four counts of King Crotchet's steps, Dragon Semibreve is said to do everything slowly, from opening his eyes, turning his head, to breathing fire. This note is demonstrated through taking one large step, with the emphasis on flowing into the next step. The step must not be so large that you are unable to take the next large step but rather, large enough to last the four counts so that it can flow into the next step, much like walking in slow motion. In the Dragon song, the step should last as long as each line, "Dragon breathe fire", "Dragon, stomp loud", "Dragon take her", "In the tower". This can also be demonstrated through clapping and moving your hands in circles away from each other. Shorter notes like King Crotchet would be quick short circles, while Lady Minim would be larger circles, clapping after 2 beats, and Dragon Semibreve would be even larger circles, clapping only after 4 beats. In our story, Knight Quaver-Crotchet spent ages trying to find the jewels until he ended up at Dragon Semibreve's lair, where he saw the secret tower. Goblin was there, trying to stop Knight Quaver-Crotchet from succeeding, but because he limped slowly, Dragon Semibreve was able to capture both Goblin and the Knight, and trap them both in the tower with the jewels.

Unicorn
The Unicorn song is written in waltz timing (3/4 time) and is a lovely way to introduce focusing on the first beat of the bar. When it is written down, music is broken up into different times (two beats, three beats or multiples of these), shown by bar lines, just like sentences have punctuation, but in performance, the music flows and it is not always easy to hear where it starts or ends. The first beat is often the strongest, and the waltz is a great way to start training the ear to hear this difference, which is a trait that research agrees is shared by all musicians. Physically, the waltz encourages this with its 'step-tip-toe, step-tip-toe' rhythm. In our story, the unicorn, who plays alone because she is self-conscious of her horn, hears the animals of the forest talking about the jewel theft and trapped Knight. Furious at this news, her horn begins to glow and she quickly decides to rescue the jewels, Knight and even Goblin. She is a lot quicker than the Dragon and quickly flies to the tower, but the Dragon is after her. Knight Quaver-Crotchet grabs the jewels and jumps on her back, but Goblin is just too slow. Just as the Dragon is about to catch her, she flies up and Goblin grabs onto her tail, escaping just in time. Everybody cheers for Unicorn back at the castle, and King Crotchet throws a party full of music, so Goblin slowly limps back to his cave, staring up at the moon to see if he can see his gold.

Continuation
It is important to physically demonstrate the continuation of the music and be ready to move to the next beat, and one way to stay ready is to keep your feet in a starting position, with the back foot on your toes, ready to go when the music starts again. Stop-start games help to develop children's abilities to recognize what will be required of them in a moment, whether walking or clapping, and the natural thrill of suspense turns the exercise into an exciting game, whether a two-year old 'surprised' expression, or a four-year old, 'guessed it right' expression.

FRANCES S. TURNBULL

Nursery Week 9 & 10

Whispering Voice

Hello Song

What you will need:

Masking tape music spots for sitting places.
Instruments and equipment out of reach.
Cover distractions with fabric.

Welcome children to Musicaliti!
Shall we practise our whispering voices:
(whisper) Do you have your whispering voice?
Let's practise our speaking voices:
(speak aloud) Do you have your speaking voice?
What about your singing voice:
(sing) Do you have your singing voice?
I think we're ready to begin!

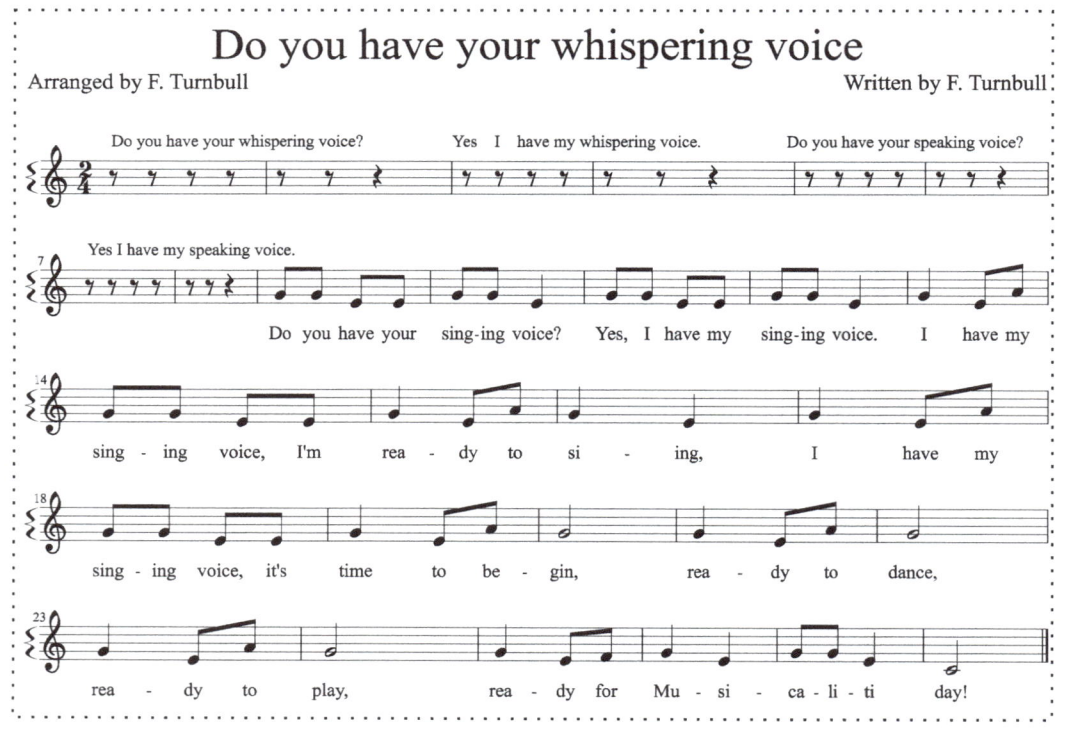

SPACE Statement

Social: The welcoming greeting routine prepares children for a new activity as well as demonstrating a better way to start the day.

Physical: Including whispering, speaking and singing allows children to experiment with communication.

Academic: Developing sensitive listening helps children to respond better to instruction and detail.

Creative: Teaching patterns develops children spatial planning and awareness.

Emotional: Routine provides emotional security by knowing what to expect.

MAGICAL MUSICAL KINGDOM: NURSERY SERIES

Nursery Week 9 & 10

Dragon
Physical Warm Up

What you will need:

Week 9 and 10: Triangle

Focus: Instrument pass-around

This week we focus on sharing and taking turns as children explore the triangle. Choose which week to play the triangle and which week to explore the physical length of the semibreve (for these purposes, the length of one bar) by taking one long step for each bar.

Look as this instrument.
Can you hear how long the sound lasts?
Let's each have a turn while we sing our dragon song.
In our story, the dragon took the jewels into his tower.
He breathed fire as he stomped slowly.
Can you pretend to breathe fire?
Then he stomped slowly, because he was very, very big.
Can you stomp like a very big dragon?
Then he collected all the jewels and took them into his tower.
Can you collect the pretend jewels to take up to your tower?
Let's sing our dragon song!

SPACE Statement

Social: The welcoming greeting routine prepares children for a new activity as well as demonstrating a better way to start the day.

Physical: Including whispering, speaking and singing allows children to experiment with communication.

Academic: Developing sensitive listening helps children to respond better to instruction and detail.

Creative: Teaching patterns develops children spatial planning and awareness.

Emotional: Routine provides emotional security by knowing what to expect.

FRANCES S. TURNBULL

Nursery Week 9&10

Do, do, pity my case

Vocal Warm Up

What you will need:

Week 9 and 10:   Sandblocks

Focus: Instrument pass-around

Continuing with our theme of sharing, we continue to pass our sandblocks around, this time focusing on passing to the beat. Demonstrate the direction of the pass and take turns inventing things to do in the dragon's garden.

> Let's play musical pass-a-long while we sing a dragon song!
> We're going to pretend that we're washing a jumper
> as we rub these sandblocks together.
> Rub, rub, rub and stop.
> Ooh, this is hard work!
> We must get it finished or the dragon won't let us out of his garden!
> Now let's wash some socks.
> Pass your sandblocks to the left (that way)
> and using our new sandblocks, rub, rub, rub and stop.
> Let's pretend we're washing different clothes
> as we sing and pass our instruments around.

SPACE Statement

Social: The welcoming greeting routine prepares children for a new activity as well as demonstrating a better way to start the day.

Physical: Including whispering, speaking and singing allows children to experiment with communication.

Academic: Developing sensitive listening helps children to respond better to instruction and detail.

Creative: Teaching patterns develops children spatial planning and awareness.

Emotional: Routine provides emotional security by knowing what to expect.

MAGICAL MUSICAL KINGDOM: NURSERY SERIES

Nursery Week 9 & 10

Dragon & Unicorn

Movement

What you will need:

Week 9 and 10:   Drum

Focus: Tapping the beat
Match the tap of the drum to the march in the feet.

The unicorn was angry with the dragon,
so angry that her horn was glowing!
They went through the town fighting and some people
gave them white bread, brown bread and even plum cake.
They had a huge fight until the unicorn flew past
the dragon, saved Knight Quaver-Crotchet and the jewels,
and took them back to the Magical Musical Kingdom.
Can you tap your drum in a marching beat?
Tap, tap, tap, and stop. March around the town as we tap.

SPACE Statement

Social: The welcoming greeting routine prepares children for a new activity as well as demonstrating a better way to start the day.

Physical: Including whispering, speaking and singing allows children to experiment with communication.

Academic: Developing sensitive listening helps children to respond better to instruction and detail.

Creative: Teaching patterns develops children spatial planning and awareness.

Emotional: Routine provides emotional security by knowing what to expect.

The Dragon and the Unicorn
Arranged by F Turnbull — Traditional

FRANCES S. TURNBULL

Nursery Week 9 & 10

Beautiful Unicorn

Instrumental Play

What you will need:

Week 9 and 10: Rhythm sticks

Focus: Rhythmic tapping

This session focuses on tapping a different rhythm to the lyrical rhythm, like horse hooves, tap-tap, tap-tap. Choose which week you want to play sticks on their own or get children to gallop to the rhythm.

Let's tap these sticks together as if they are a horse,
galloping through the field.
Tap-tap, tap-tap, tap-tap and stop.
Now let's tap like a trotting horse,
tap-tap-tap-tap, tap-tap-tap-tap and stop.
Choose whether you want to do galloping or trotting
as we sing about a unicorn that hides in the valley,
but then has to go and save the family.

SPACE Statement

Social: The welcoming greeting routine prepares children for a new activity as well as demonstrating a better way to start the day.

Physical: Including whispering, speaking and singing allows children to experiment with communication.

Academic: Developing sensitive listening helps children to respond better to instruction and detail.

Creative: Teaching patterns develops children spatial planning and awareness.

Emotional: Routine provides emotional security by knowing what to expect.

MAGICAL MUSICAL KINGDOM: NURSERY SERIES

Dragon & Unicorn
Story/Investigation

Nursery Week 9 & 10

SPACE Statement

What you will need:

Week 9 and 10:   Pictures and characters
Depending on time allowance and group, act out the story.
Are you ready for a story?
It's quite exciting, and every week, we hear a bit more!
This is a picture of the Magical Musical Kingdom.
Let's rub our ears and get them ready to listen.

A long time ago in a Magical Musical Kingdom far away, there lived King Crotchet married to Queen Quaver, protected by the brave and handsome Knight Quaver-Crotchet, who was married to Lady Minim, who looked after the animals and lived together with Princess Semiquaver and Frog Prince, but Goblin had stolen the King's jewels and Flying Fairy had hung Goblin's gold on a moon beam as punishment. Now Knight Quaver-Crotchet was getting further away from the Kingdom, the castle was far away because he was getting nearer to the lair of Dragon Semibreve. Everything Dragon Semibreve did was slow because he was so big. He opened his eyes slowly, he walked slowly and even blew fire out slowly. When Dragon Semibreve blew fire out, everything would start shaking altogether, his arms and legs, tummy and tail, until he stopped. Dragon Semibreve didn't like things that moved fast, so when Goblin took the jewels to the tower, he had to creep very quietly. Knight Quaver-Crotchet moved very quickly and before he knew what had happened, Dragon Semibreve had trapped him in the tower with the jewels and Goblin. The dreadful news travelled over the Magical Musical Kingdom until a beautiful dancing Unicorn, alone in a field, heard the sad tale. She always played on her own, dancing every single day, but when she heard the news, Unicorn's horn began to glow, which meant that she was very cross. Shaking out her golden wings, she flew straight to Dragon Semibreve's tower and very quickly, Knight Quaver-Crotchet took the jewels and jumped on her back. Goblin took so long to creep to the window that he could only hold onto Unicorn's tail, as they flew through the fiery mountains and back to the castle. King Crotchet was so pleased to have his Magical Musical Kingdom restored that he threw a huge party. There was so much music that Goblin crept away back to his cave and sometimes, when the sky is right, you can see that the moon still looks a little golden, where Flying Fairy hung Goblin's gold on the moonbeam.

Social: The welcoming greeting routine prepares children for a new activity as well as demonstrating a better way to start the day.

Physical: Including whispering, speaking and singing allows children to experiment with communication.

Academic: Developing sensitive listening helps children to respond better to instruction and detail.

Creative: Teaching patterns develops children spatial planning and awareness.

Emotional: Routine provides emotional security by knowing what to expect.

Nursery Week 9&10

Dragon & Unicorn
Instrumental

What you will need:

Week 9: None
Track length: 1.58 (One-eyed Maestro, K.McCleod)

This time is for creative expression without talking. Begin by clapping as the main music line in this song begins faster (claps) then the music line changes to slower flutes (walking) and repeats.

We are showing that the change in tempo changes the mood of the music; the slower tempo is more relaxed and the faster tempo is more intense.

Week 10: None
Track length: 1.20 (Happy Alley, K. McCleod)

This time is for creative expression without talking. Demonstrate responding to each key change by starting with skipping, then clapping, and knee-tapping when the music changes, then back to skipping. In this song, we are emphasizing the difference that a change in key makes in the feel of a song by changing our response from legs to arms.

It's time to listen to music
and find a creative way to respond.
Be sure to listen to how the music sounds,
whether it is high or low, quick or slow,
and try to copy it.
Let's find lots of different ways
to respond to the music.

SPACE Statement

Social: The welcoming greeting routine prepares children for a new activity as well as demonstrating a better way to start the day.

Physical: Including whispering, speaking and singing allows children to experiment with communication.

Academic: Developing sensitive listening helps children to respond better to instruction and detail.

Creative: Teaching patterns develops children spatial planning and awareness.

Emotional: Routine provides emotional security by knowing what to expect.

MAGICAL MUSICAL KINGDOM: NURSERY SERIES

Nursery Week 9 & 10

Goodbye

Goodbye Song

What you will need:

Week 1 and 2:   Sit in circle to sing goodbye.

The recording can be used when singing to younger children who won't sing back yet. Stop after "but now it's time to say" so that you can sing to each child, and wait for them to sing back their response. This is a perfect opportunity to determine whether children are singing in tune on their own.

If stickers have been used as rewards for behaviour during the session, this is also the time to ensure that each child receives a sticker, showing each child that you value them equally.

What an exciting day we've had,
playing Kings and Queens!
It's time to go, so let's get our
waving hands ready
as we get ready to sing goodbye.

SPACE Statement

Social: The welcoming greeting routine prepares children for a new activity as well as demonstrating a better way to start the day.

Physical: Including whispering, speaking and singing allows children to experiment with communication.

Academic: Developing sensitive listening helps children to respond better to instruction and detail.

Creative: Teaching patterns develops children spatial planning and awareness.

Emotional: Routine provides emotional security by knowing what to expect.

FRANCES S. TURNBULL

Nursery Week 11 & 12

6 SUMMARY WEEKS

Final weeks

Depending on the length of the term, you may have more weeks beyond the 10 characters of the story. It finishes the series nicely, and acts as a fun reminder, to go through the entire story in one musical sitting, even using it as a mini-performance for parents. Depending on the number of weeks remaining (usually 2 in a twelve week term), you may choose or like to get the children to choose their favourite song from each character, as each character has two songs, usually one is instrumental and the other is a dance or a game. The second week could include the songs that were left out the previous week, to revise al the songs in the series.

One of the most enjoyable ways to end this series is with a mini-performance for parents. Not only can parents see what their children have accomplished, it gives them greater insight into the background of the handouts that they have received each week. This also gives children the opportunity to dress up and perform something familiar to the people they love without the pressure of remembering words or doing the right steps; essentially, it is one big, fun game. Props can be as elaborate or as minimal as your budget or imagination allow, while each character could easily be a number of children where groups are bigger than ten.

The final weeks are also useful in identifying the musical connections between the characters, as these notes come up each week, helping children to become completely familiar with the notes and rhythms well before they pick up their first instrument. Similar notes can be picked out of the printed music on the handouts, and games can be invented with simpler tunes, working on pitching them in the right order (e.g. paper plates on the floor).

MAGICAL MUSICAL KINGDOM: NURSERY SERIES

Nursery Week 11 & 12

Whispering Voice

Hello Song

What you will need:

Masking tape music spots for sitting places.
Instruments and equipment out of reach.
Cover distractions with fabric.

Welcome children to Musicaliti!
Shall we practise our whispering voices:
(whisper) Do you have your whispering voice?
Let's practise our speaking voices:
(speak aloud) Do you have your speaking voice?
What about your singing voice:
(sing) Do you have your singing voice?
I think we're ready to begin!

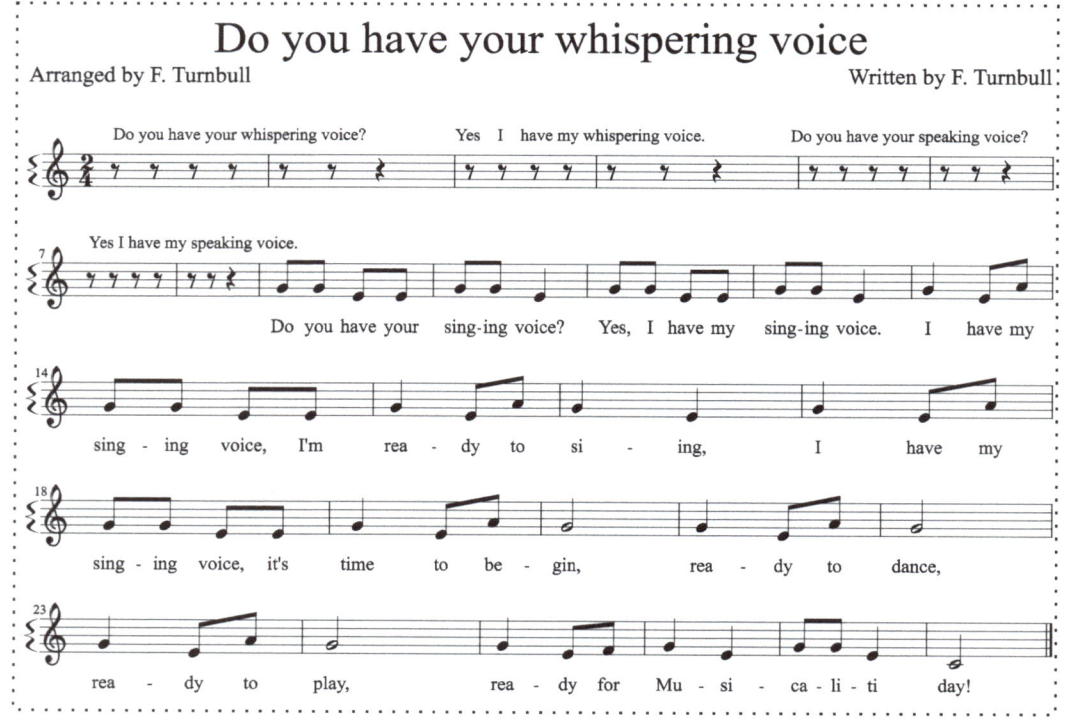

SPACE Statement

Social: The welcoming greeting routine prepares children for a new activity as well as demonstrating a better way to start the day.

Physical: Including whispering, speaking and singing allows children to experiment with communication.

Academic: Developing sensitive listening helps children to respond better to instruction and detail.

Creative: Teaching patterns develops children spatial planning and awareness.

Emotional: Routine provides emotional security by knowing what to expect.

Nursery Week 11 & 12

Final Weeks

Summary Time

What you will need:

Week 11 and 12:   Choose the children's favourite songs

Week 11	Week 12
Old King Glory or *Queens are Royal* (Movement)	*I am King* or *Queen of Hearts* (Instrumental)
Knight & Horse or *Down came my Friend* (Instrumental)	*Duke of York* or *Pink Hat* (Movement)
Semiquaver or *Little Bells* (Movement)	*Built my Princess* or *Hopping Hopping* (Instrumental)
Goblin or *Love Somebody* (Instrumental)	*Goblin Protector* or *Flying Fairy* (Movement)
Dragon or *Dragon and the Unicorn* (Movement)	*Do Pity my Case* or *Beautiful Unicorn* (Instrumental)
Favourite piece (e.g. *Electrodoodle*) (Creative Movement)	Favourite piece (e.g. *Happy Ally*) (Creative Movement)

SPACE Statement

Social: The welcoming greeting routine prepares children for a new activity as well as demonstrating a better way to start the day.

Physical: Including whispering, speaking and singing allows children to experiment with communication.

Academic: Developing sensitive listening helps children to respond better to instruction and detail.

Creative: Teaching patterns develops children spatial planning and awareness.

Emotional: Routine provides emotional security by knowing what to expect.

MAGICAL MUSICAL KINGDOM: NURSERY SERIES

Nursery Week 11 & 12

Goodbye

Goodbye Song

What you will need:

Week 1 and 2:   Sit in circle to sing goodbye.

The recording can be used when singing to younger children who won't sing back yet. Stop after "but now it's time to say" so that you can sing to each child, and wait for them to sing back their response. This is a perfect opportunity to determine whether children are singing in tune on their own.

If stickers have been used as rewards for behaviour during the session, this is also the time to ensure that each child receives a sticker, showing each child that you value them equally.

> What an exciting day we've had,
> playing Kings and Queens!
> It's time to go, so let's get our
> waving hands ready
> as we get ready to sing goodbye.

SPACE Statement

Social: The welcoming greeting routine prepares children for a new activity as well as demonstrating a better way to start the day.

Physical: Including whispering, speaking and singing allows children to experiment with communication.

Academic: Developing sensitive listening helps children to respond better to instruction and detail.

Creative: Teaching patterns develops children spatial planning and awareness.

Emotional: Routine provides emotional security by knowing what to expect.

FRANCES S. TURNBULL

7 HANDOUTS

Why Handouts?
This series includes handouts sheets for each of the characters as a reminder of the music series this term. Pictures of the characters are included on the handouts next to the title, and the notes represented are also included so that children become familiar and more comfortable with music notation.

Handouts act as useful reminders for children and conversation points for parents of children who may be less vocal than others. Musically-trained parents may be able to pick out the tune, while non-musical parents will be able to read the words, potentially reminding their child of the tune. Children will certainly be reminded by the exciting story included with each handout. With most songs written in the anhemitonic pentatonic scale, songs extend only five notes (excluding notes with semi tones), making it easier for children to learn and sing successfully.

In addition to the handouts, a colour page of characters has been included and may be reproduced for storytelling, as well as an A4 colour picture, where the story of the Magical Musical Kingdom takes place, as a background for the characters.

Notation practice
Musical knowledge may also be consolidated using the hand out sheets which may be photocopied. The 'Make your own rhythm' pages can be copied, cut and laminated so that children can create rhythms of songs they already sing, or to create new rhythms to clap or tap. The rhythm lines are in 4/4 time so that each line can have four counts (gaps are rests). The notation used on the lines may be musical or insect depending on the children.

A quick reminder of the notation values:

Semibreve	Snail	4 counts	(1 on a line)
Minim	Worm	2 counts	(2 on a line)
Crotchet	Bee	1 count	(4 on a line)
Quaver	Spider	1 count	(4 on a line)
Semiquaver	Caterpillar	1 count	(4 on a line)
Dotted quaver semiquaver	Beetle	1 count	(4 on a line)
Semiquaver dotted quaver	The ant	1 count	(4 on a line)
Triplet	Butterfly	1 count	(4 on a line)
Quaver semiquaver	Hamburger	1 count	(4 on a line)
Semiquaver quaver	Sausages	1 count	(4 on a line)

I am King

Arranged by F. Turnbull
Written by F. Turnbull

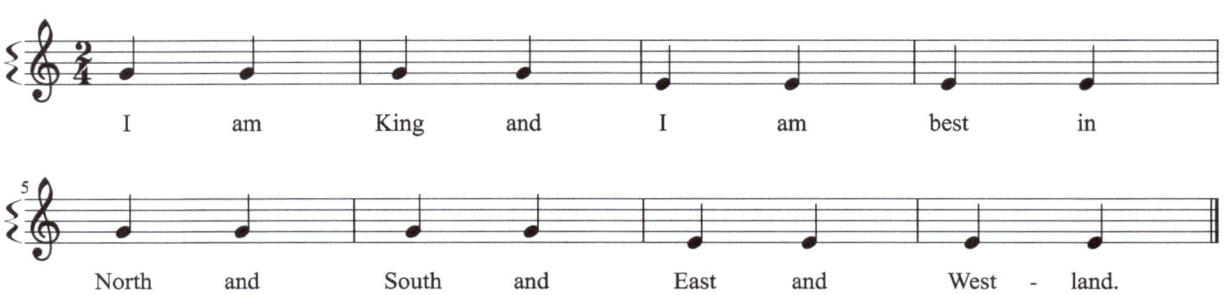

A long time ago in a Magical Musical Kingdom far away, there lived King Crotchet. King Crotchet was big and strong and when he walked past, everyone stopped to watch him because he was so loud and took such big steps. King Crotchet ruled wisely and justly and had a great crown full of every precious stone in the world. People loved King Crotchet so much that they travelled far and wide to find the most precious stone and every week, he would choose the best new precious stones to add to his crown. The rest of the precious stones were added to the walls of his magnificent castle that shone each morning on the magical hill. Every day King Crotchet loved to play croquet, a game where he would hit four balls though four hoops in the ground.

Old King Glory

Arranged by F Turnbull
Traditional

MAY BE REPRODUCED FOR EDUCATIONAL PURPOSES ONLY

Queen Quaver
Queens are Royal

Arranged by F. Turnbull　　　　　　　　　　　　　　　　　　　Written by F. Turnbull

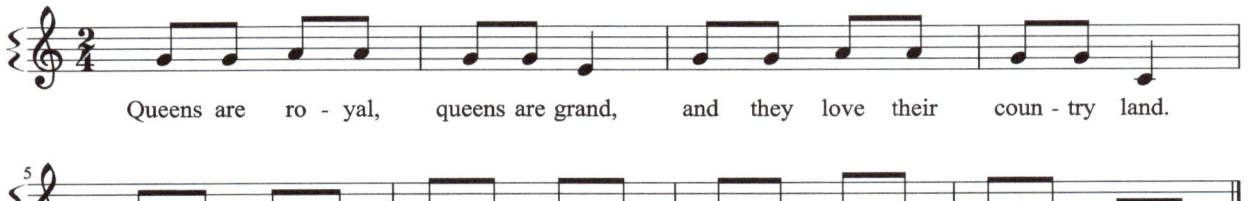

A long time ago in a Magical Musical Kingdom far away, there lived King Crotchet. King Crotchet was married to Queen Quaver. Queen Quaver moved quickly and quietly, and was always stepped ahead of the King. Queen Quaver was very beautiful, the most beautiful lady in the land, and people travelled from all over the world to see her. Wherever she went, the mountains peaked higher, the grass shone greener, the flowers grew brighter and even the rivers shone until they glistened, although she hardly made a sound. Queen Quaver loved to play tennis and would always bounce and hit the ball as quickly as she could.

The Queen of Hearts

Arranged by F Turnbull　　　　　　　　　　　　　　　　　　　　　　Traditional

MAY BE REPRODUCED FOR EDUCATIONAL PURPOSES ONLY

Knight Quaver-Crotchet
Knight and Horse

Arranged by F. Turnbull
Written by F. Turnbull

Knight and horse ride fier-cely, fier-cely,
Knight and horse move quick-ly, quick-ly.
Ne-ver ti-ring, bra-vely, bra-vely,
Save King and slay beas-tie, beas-tie.

A long time ago in a Magical Musical Kingdom far away, there lived King Crotchet married to Queen Quaver. They lived with a brave and handsome Knight Quaver-Crotchet. He was the most brave person in all the land and would do anything to protect his King Crotchet and Queen Quaver. When bad people took things from the King, Knight Quaver-Crotchet would travel to the other side of the world and never give up until they were caught. He wasn't scared of anything or anyone because he was fit and well trained. When he was training, Knight Quaver-Crotchet loved to fence, a sport with swords that relied on cunning and expertise.

Grand Old Duke of York

Arranged by F Turnbull
Traditional

Oh, the grand old duke of York, he had ten thou-sand men, he
marched them up to the top of the hill and he marched them down a-
gain. And when they were up, they were up, and
when they were down, they were down, and when they were on-ly
half-way up they were nei-ther up nor down.

MAY BE REPRODUCED FOR EDUCATIONAL PURPOSES ONLY

Lady Minim

Pink Hat Lady

Arranged by F. Turnbull
Written by F. Turnbull

Pink hat, Pink shoes, posh frock, read news, nod and sip tea, lift hat, curt-sey.

A long time ago in a Magical Musical Kingdom far away, there lived King Crotchet married to Queen Quaver, protected by the brave and handsome Knight Quaver-Crotchet. Knight Quaver-Crotchet was married to Lady Minim, a very special Lady who was very good at caring for sick animals. Lady Minim moved slowly and calmly so that they were never startled or afraid and some people said she could even speak the secret language of animals. When she wasn't caring for animals, Lady Minim loved to play bowls, gently rolling one ball to hit the bull's eye.

Down Came a Lady

Arranged by F Turnbull
Traditional

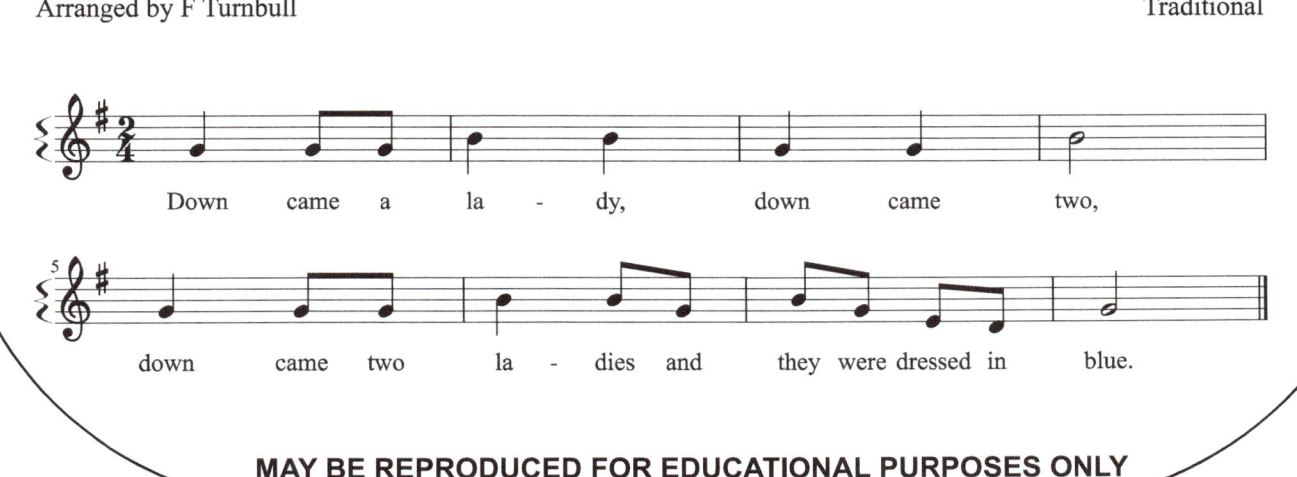

Down came a lady, down came two, down came two la-dies and they were dressed in blue.

MAY BE REPRODUCED FOR EDUCATIONAL PURPOSES ONLY

Princess Semiquaver

Princess Semiquaver

Arranged by F. Turnbull Written by F. Turnbull

Se - mi - qua - ver plays in the mea - dow,
se - mi - qua - ver plays in the ri - ver,
Se - mi - qua - ver found lit - tle frog and
kissed him; there a prince stood.

A long time ago in a Magical Musical Kingdom far away, there lived King Crotchet married to Queen Quaver, protected by the brave and handsome Knight Quaver-Crotchet who was married to Lady Minim who looked after the animals. In this household lived the King's most precious jewel, his daughter, Princess Semiquaver. Semiquaver moved even more quickly than the Queen and was often running quickly or spinning in fields, forests and near ponds with all the animals of the Kingdom. Starting very quietly she got louder and louder as she got further away from the Castle. One day when she was at the pond, she saw a little frog. He had a beautiful golden head and she thought he looked like a little prince so she called him Frog Prince.

Built my Princess

Arranged by F Turnbull Traditional

Built my Prin - cess a fine brick house, Built it in a gar - den, I
put her in but she jumped out so fare thee we - ll my dar - lin'.

MAY BE REPRODUCED FOR EDUCATIONAL PURPOSES ONLY

Frog Prince

Hopping Hopping

Arranged by F. Turnbull Written by F. Turnbull

Hop-ping hop-ping on a log, I'm a hop-ping lit-tle frog.

Kiss, kiss, kiss, now I am a prince!

A long time ago in a Magical Musical Kingdom far away, there lived King Crotchet married to Queen Quaver, protected by the brave and handsome Knight Quaver-Crotchet who was married to Lady Minim who looked after the animals and lived together with Princess Semiquaver. Princess Semiquaver always visited Frog Prince with a juicy bug and one day, Frog Prince did a froggy somersault trick. She laughed out loud, and thought he was so clever that she gave him a kiss. Poof! Suddenly he disappeared and a handsome prince appeared in his place, from a spell that a naughty Goblin put on him. The prince loved his new name so much that he was known by everyone as Frog Prince. He used to croak very loudly when he was a frog, and was so glad that now he could speak quietly, too. His favourite sport was horse riding and now that he was a person again, Frog Prince could ride his horse.

The Little Bells

Arranged by F Turnbull Traditional

The lit-tle bells of West-min-ster go ding dong, ding dong dong.

MAY BE REPRODUCED FOR EDUCATIONAL PURPOSES ONLY

Arranged by F. Turnbull

Written by F. Turnbull

Gob - lin, gob - lin, cree - ping, snea - king, stole the King's jewels, now in hi - ding.

A long time ago in a Magical Musical Kingdom far away, there lived King Crotchet married to Queen Quaver, protected by the brave and handsome Knight Quaver-Crotchet who was married to Lady Minim who looked after the animals and lived together with Princess Semiquaver and Frog Prince. But far away from the Magical Kingdom, in a dark and dreary cave full of broken instruments lived Goblin, the naughty, creeping goblin who turned Frog Prince into a frog. He didn't like musical instruments, only the sound of voices and when he was cross he crept around and broke all the instruments he could find. He was very cross with Princess Semiquaver for changing him back so he did another magic spell and crept into the castle and put the Kings' jewels in a secret tower, far away from the castle. Princess Semiquaver was very sad and King Crotchet and Frog Prince were furious. Queen Quaver and Lady Minim asked Knight Quaver-Crotchet to please find the jewels so Knight Quaver-Crotchet left immediately to search every tower in the land to find them.

Goblin Protector

Arranged by F Turnbull

Traditional

Gob - lin Pro - tec - tor was dressed in all green, Gob - lin Pro - tec - tor was sent to the Queen, The Queen did not like him, no more did the King, so Gob - lin Pro - tec - tor was sent back a - gain.

MAY BE REPRODUCED FOR EDUCATIONAL PURPOSES ONLY

Skipping Flying Fairy

Arranged by F. Turnbull
Written by F. Turnbull

Skip - ping, fly - ing, o - ver the woods,
Gob - lin's gold, he's up - to no good,
Skip - ping, fly - ing way up high,
Hang gold on a moon - beam high.

A long time ago in a Magical Musical Kingdom far away, there lived King Crotchet married to Queen Quaver, protected by the brave and handsome Knight Quaver-Crotchet who was married to Lady Minim who looked after the animals and lived together with Princess Semiquaver and Frog Prince but Goblin had stolen the King's jewels. While Knight Quaver-Crotchet was searching every tower in the land, he came across Flying Fairy, who flew everywhere. He searched her tower, but Princess Semiquaver just wasn't there. When he told Flying Fairy what Goblin had done and how sad Frog Prince was, Flying Fairy got very cross indeed. She never spoke, but played music because she was surrounded by every instrument in the world. She wanted to teach Gobin a lesson so using her special magic, she flew to his dark cave and saw all the broken instruments. Right at the back of the cave was a very shiny pot of gold, hidden behind a tree stump. Flying Fairy picked it up and flew right to the moon and hung it on a moon beam as punishment!

Love Somebody

Arranged by F Turnbull
Traditional

Love some - bo - dy, yes I do, Love some - bo - dy, yes I do,
Love some - bo - dy yes, I do, Love some - bo - dy but I won't say who
Love some - bo - dy, yes I do, Love some - bo - dy, yes I do,
Love some - bo - dy yes I do, Love some - bo - dy and it's you, you, you.

MAY BE REPRODUCED FOR EDUCATIONAL PURPOSES ONLY

Dragon
Dragon

Arranged by F. Turnbull
Written by F. Turnbull

Dra - gon breathe fire, dra - gon, stomp loud, dra - gon take her In the to - wer.

A long time ago in a Magical Musical Kingdom far away, there lived King Crotchet married to Queen Quaver, protected by the brave and handsome Knight Quaver-Crotchet who was married to Lady Minim who looked after the animals and lived together with Princess Semiquaver and Frog Prince but Goblin had stolen the King's jewels and Flying Fairy had hung Goblin's gold on a moon beam as punishment. Now Knight Quaver-Crotchet was getting further away from the Kingdom, the castle was far away because he was getting nearer to the lair of Dragon Semibreve. Everything Dragon Semibreve did was slow because he was so big. He opened his eyes slowly, he walked slowly and even blew fire out slowly. When Dragon Semibreve blew fire out, everything would start shaking altogether, his arms and legs, tummy and tail, until he stopped. Dragon Semibreve didn't like things that moved fast, so when Goblin took the jewels to the tower, he had to creep very quietly. Knight Quaver-Crotchet moved very quickly and before he knew what had happened, Dragon Semibreve had trapped him in the tower with the jewels and Goblin.

Do, Do, Pity my Case

Arranged by F Turnbull
Traditional

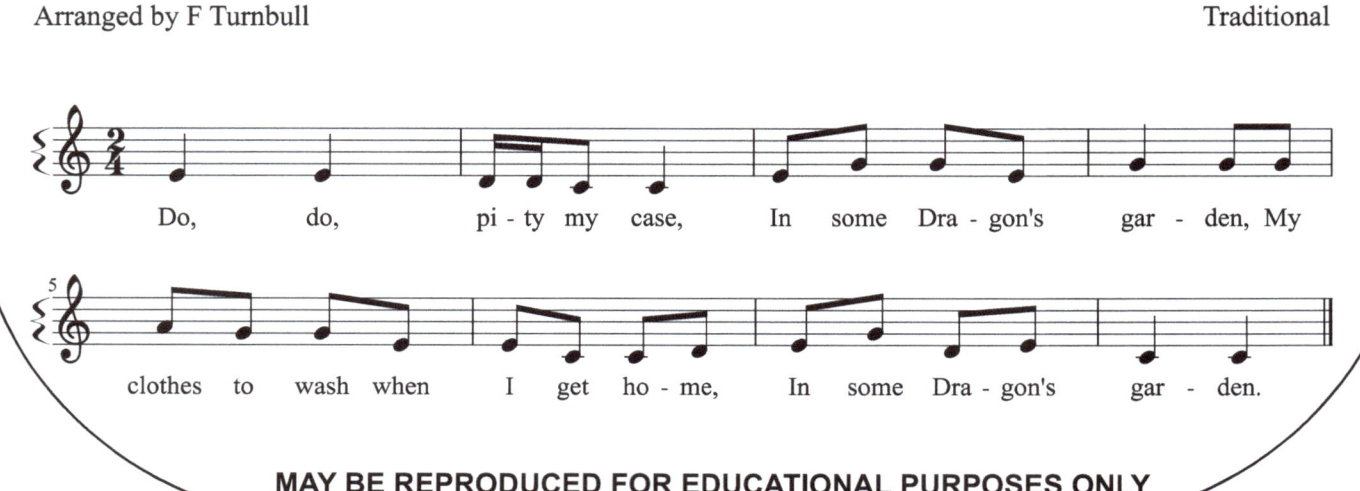

Do, do, pi - ty my case, In some Dra - gon's gar - den, My clothes to wash when I get ho - me, In some Dra - gon's gar - den.

MAY BE REPRODUCED FOR EDUCATIONAL PURPOSES ONLY

Beautiful Unicorn

Arranged by F. Turnbull
Written by F. Turnbull

Beau-ti-ful u-ni-corn, where do you   In the val-ley.
Beau-ti-ful u-ni-corn, let's take a ride! Save the fam'-ly.

A long time ago in a Magical Musical Kingdom far away, there lived King Crotchet married to Queen Quaver, protected by the brave and handsome Knight Quaver-Crotchet who was married to Lady Minim who looked after the animals and lived together with Princess Semiquaver and Frog Prince but Goblin had stolen the King's jewels and Flying Fairy had hung Goblin's gold on a moon beam as punishment while Dragon Semibreve trapped Knight Quaver-Crotchet and Goblin with the jewels in his fiery tower. The dreadful news travelled over the Magical Musical Kingdom until a beautiful dancing Unicorn, alone in a field, heard the sad tale. She always played on his own, dancing every single day, but when she heard the news, Unicorn's horn began to glow, which meant that she was very cross. Shaking out her golden wings, she flew straight to Dragon Semibreve's tower and very quickly, Knight Quaver-Crotchet took the jewels and jumped on her back. Goblin took so long to creep to the window that he could only hold onto Unicorn's tail, as they flew through the fiery mountains and back to the castle. King Crotchet was so pleased to have his Magical Musical Kingdom restored that he threw a huge party. There was so much music that Goblin crept away back to his cave and sometimes, when the sky is right, you can see that the moon still looks a little golden, where Flying Fairy hung Goblin's gold on the moonbeam.

The Dragon and the Unicorn

Arranged by F Turnbull
Traditional

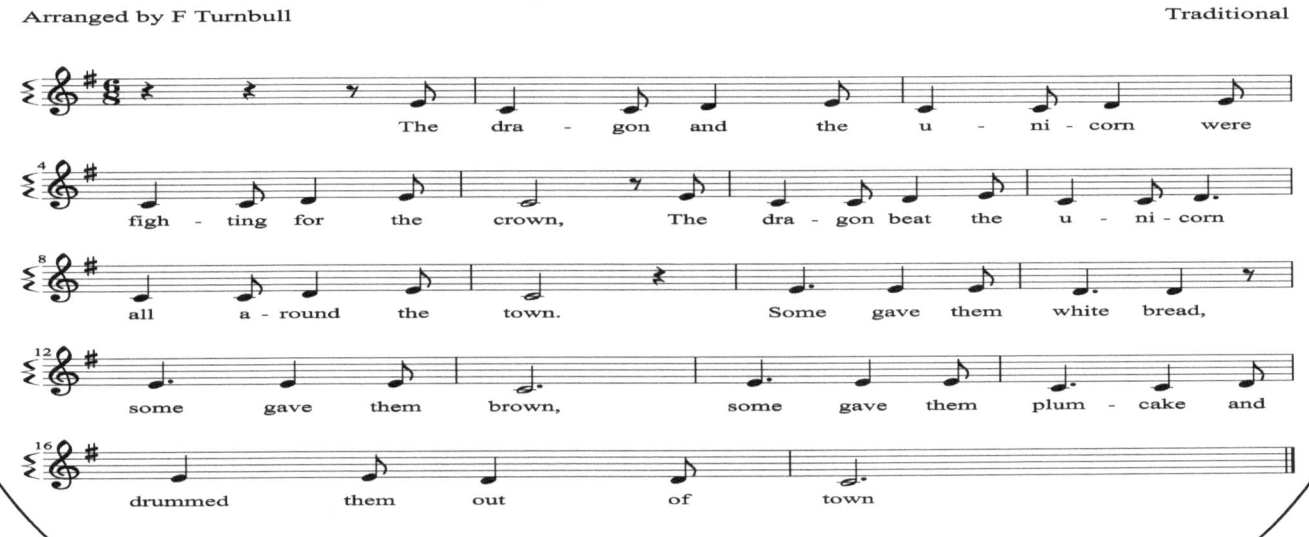

The dra-gon and the u-ni-corn were figh-ting for the crown, The dra-gon beat the u-ni-corn all a-round the town. Some gave them white bread, some gave them brown, some gave them plum-cake and drummed them out of town

MAY BE REPRODUCED FOR EDUCATIONAL PURPOSES ONLY

MAGICAL MUSICAL KINGDOM: NURSERY SERIES

Character Pictures: copy, cut and laminate

MAY BE REPRODUCED FOR EDUCATIONAL PURPOSES ONLY

MAGICAL MUSICAL KINGDOM: NURSERY SERIES

Make your own rhythms:

Cut out notes and insects and place them on the rhythm line.

MAY BE REPRODUCED FOR EDUCATIONAL PURPOSES ONLY

FRANCES S. TURNBULL

Make your own Rhythms:

| 4 |
| 4 |

| 4 |
| 4 |

| 4 |
| 4 |

| 4 |
| 4 |

Cut out notes and insects and place them on the rhythm line.

MAY BE REPRODUCED FOR EDUCATIONAL PURPOSES ONLY

MAGICAL MUSICAL KINGDOM: NURSERY SERIES

Make your own Rhythms:

4
4

4
4

4
4

4
4

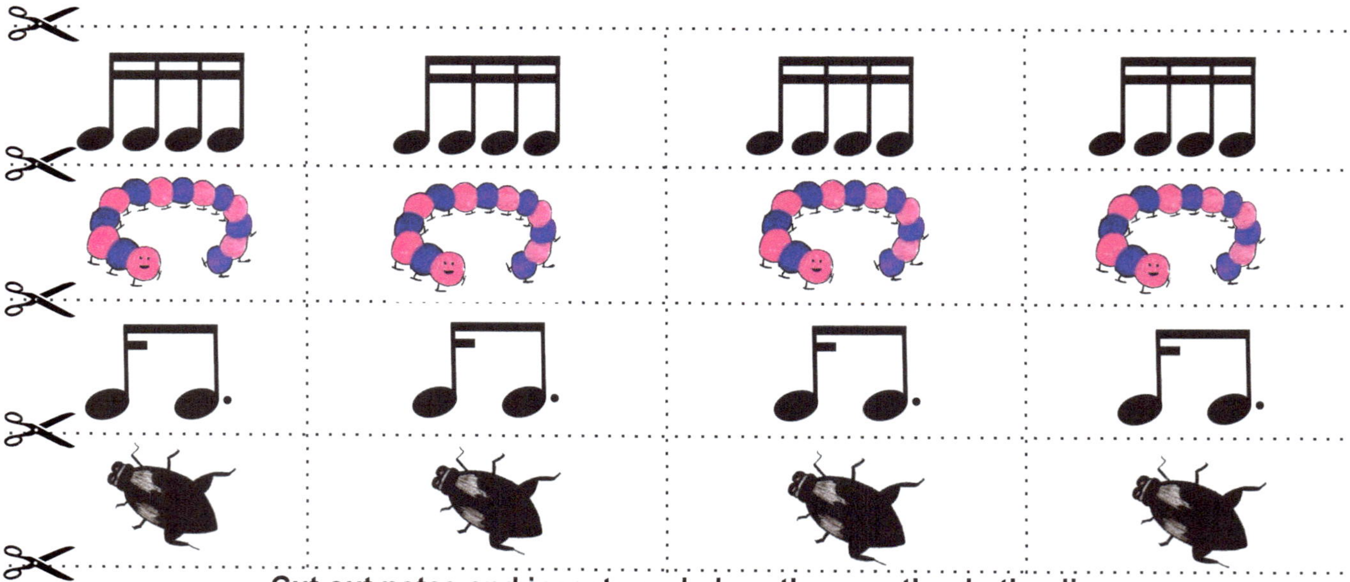

Cut out notes and insects and place them on the rhythm line.

MAY BE REPRODUCED FOR EDUCATIONAL PURPOSES ONLY

FRANCES S. TURNBULL

Make your own Rhythms:

4
4

4
4

4
4

4
4

Cut out notes and insects and place them on the rhythm line.

MAY BE REPRODUCED FOR EDUCATIONAL PURPOSES ONLY

Make your own Rhythms:

4
4

4
4

4
4

4
4

Cut out notes and insects and place them on the rhythm line.

MAY BE REPRODUCED FOR EDUCATIONAL PURPOSES ONLY

AVAILABLE TITLES:

Musicaliti Nursery: Round and Round is a full-colour, illustrated book of well known children's songs for children. Each song includes music rhythms to which children can clap, tap, walk and sing.
ISBN: 978-1-907-935-008

FORTHCOMING TITLES:

Musicaliti Nursery Series: Sharks, Fish, Shells is a full-colour, teaching series of well known and original children's songs with a fishy element. Sessions include suggested instruments and activities, with an optional CD of music to purchase or download.
ISBN: 978-1-907-935-169

Musicaliti Nursery Series: Balloons, Candles, Cake is a full-colour, teaching series of well known and original children's songs with a party element. Sessions include suggested instruments and activities, with an optional CD of music to purchase or download.
ISBN: 978-1-907-935-190

Musicaliti Nursery Series: Car, bike, plane is a full-colour, teaching series of well known and original children's songs with a transport element. Sessions include suggested instruments and activities, with an optional CD of music to purchase or download.

ISBN: 978-1-907-935-213

Follow *Musicaliti* on Facebook, LInked in, Reverb Nation, SoundCloud, Twitter and YouTube!

ABOUT THE AUTHOR

Frances has presented early years music sessions in a variety of settings since 2006, after training as a secondary mathematics and science teacher. She is fascinated by research into the health, educational and developmental benefits of music. Not content with being involved with children's music alone, she co-directs a local community choir, the Breightmet Warblers.

www.ingramcontent.com/pod-product-compliance
Lightning Source LLC
Chambersburg PA
CBHW042018150426
43197CB00002B/63